CU00924389

Focus
on Faith

A resource for the journey
into the Catholic Church

DEBORAH M. JONES
MICHAEL GRIFFIN

Kevin
Mayhew

First published in 1987 by KEVIN MAYHEW LTD
Buxhall, Stowmarket, Suffolk IP14 3BW
Email: info@kevinmayhewltd.com

This revised edition © 1996 Kevin Mayhew Limited

The right of Deborah M. Jones to be identified as the author
of this work has been asserted by her in accordance
with the Copyright, Designs and Patents Act 1988.

All rights reserved. No part of this publication may be reproduced,
stored in a retrieval system, or transmitted, in any form or by any
means, electronic, mechanical, photocopying, recording or
otherwise, without prior written permission of the publisher.

All Scripture texts are taken (with a few clearly indicated
exceptions) from The Jerusalem Bible, published and copyright
1966, 1967, and 1968 by Darton, Longman and Todd Ltd and
Doubleday & Co Inc, and are used by permission of the
publishers. Other quotations from copyright material are
credited in the Acknowledgements on page 144.

Photographs: © Carlos Reyes/Andes Press Agency
Drawings: Christine Pilsworth
Cartoons: Arthur Baker

9 8 7 6 5 4 3 2

ISBN 1 86209 887 4
Catalogue No 1500074

Edited by Peter Dainty
Cover design by Jonathan Stroulger
Typesetting by Louise Hill

Printed in Great Britain

CONTENTS

The authors

Deborah M. Jones was born in Cheshire and studied at University College, Cardiff, Leeds University and Regina Mundi Pontifical Institute in Rome. For many years she worked in full-time adult religious education in the Diocese of East Anglia, and acted as Deputy Editor of the monthly journal *Priests & People*. She serves on the Bishops' Conference Committee for Theology and is co-Chair of the Association of Adult Religious Educators.

She is now Editor of the *Catholic Herald*.

Michael Griffin studied for the priesthood at the English College, Rome. He is a priest in the Diocese of East Anglia, having served in Peterborough, Northants, and Hadleigh in Suffolk. His special interest is adult catechesis.

Special thanks to Mgr Anthony Philpot S.T.L. for his helpful comments on the text, and to the clergy and laity of East Anglia for their generous support and friendship.

INTRODUCTION

One after another, parishes throughout the world are adopting the thinking and practice of the R.C.I.A. – the Rite of Christian Initiation of Adults. At once ancient and new, this Rite expresses the essential mission and purpose of the Church – to draw all people to the Father through Christ Jesus the Son, in the power of the Holy Spirit.

New members of the Church are led, by stages and at their own pace, into full participation with the community of the faithful alongside whom they have journeyed. That community develops its proper identity – as an evangelising, welcoming, faith-sustaining body.

There is a time between two of the liturgical rites, the Rite of Entry or of 'becoming catechumens' and the Rite of Election or Enrolment (when the Church formally 'elects' the candidates to progress to full initiation, and the 'elected ones' express their will to accept membership of the Catholic Church). This time, called the 'catechumenate' is designated for the systematic exploration of the thinking and practice of Catholic Christianity.

This book is primarily intended to help those parishes in which people are embarking on the catechumenate period of the R.C.I.A., or those who would like a change in the materials they are using. Ideas and suggestions are given here for candidates, their friends and sponsors, group leaders and other parishioners, for use during this period.

Further information about the R.C.I.A. is given at the end of the book.

The process

The book is divided into units of material for twenty sessions. These can be taken in any order.

Before each session, the text for the next unit should be read at home.

Begin each session by reviewing the text of the unit – especially as some participants may not have had the opportunity of reading it in advance. An important part of the reviewing process is in inviting and answering questions. A copy of the *Catechism of the Catholic Church* may be useful for reference.

Then move on to the suggestions for Large Group and Small Group work – adapt them to suit your group.

Each session concludes with a short period of prayer. The material has been designed with the needs of the average 'ordinary' parish in mind – in the hope that nobody is offended by that description!

To allow for maximum flexibility, references to the liturgical seasons are not included; neither are references to the Rites (there is nothing better than the Rites themselves!).

A note for Catholic members of the course

Three golden rules for fruitful faith-sharing groups

It will help the catechumens, and yourselves, if you can cultivate the following:

1. Be a good friend: be friendly and welcoming; take the initiative in 'breaking the ice'; invite the catechumens to your home for coffee or a meal; see that no one is prevented from attending because he/she needs a lift, or a baby-sitter; share some of the chores and projects.

2. Be a good listener: pay real attention to what others are saying, rather than preparing your own 'tuppenny's worth'! Hogging the floor, or flooding people with information can be really off-putting.

3. Be respectful: on two levels – never try to belittle or insult another's past, background or beliefs; and always respect the other person's doubts and difficulties. If you try to force an opinion on someone, they will walk away. If they want to walk away for any reason, they must be free to do so.

BE REAL . . . BE RESPECTFUL . . . BE FRIENDLY . . .
After all, don't *you* prefer others to be so?

Resource

This book is simply *one* resource in a process which takes account of the needs and development of each individual. The process itself has to be flexible and adaptable. No one resource could pretend to answer all the questions about Catholic life and belief. The most important resource is the living witness and testimony of the many good and faithful Catholics to be found in every parish.

This book is for
- catechumens and their sponsors
- candidates for full reception into the Catholic Church
- returning Catholics who may have been away from church for many years
- the team of catechists, group leaders and helpers
- friends and supporters of the above from the Catholic parish

Group session

A note about terms used:

All the people at the meeting constitute the **Large Group**. If you can divide this into even two or more groups of three to seven people, you have the **Small Groups** in which the personal sharing takes place. Each Small Group requires a **Small Group Leader** who sees to it that everyone has the opportunity to participate freely. The over-all **Team Leader** or **Co-ordinator**, who may or may not be a priest, will need to share the responsibility for the course with a **Team**, to include the Small Group Leaders; those responsible for **hospitality**, e.g. the host/ess, tea-makers, caretaker; those who will be **Session Leaders**, i.e. in charge for a Session – reviewing the text at the beginning of the unit for that session, time-keeping and anything else which may need to be done to ensure that the session runs smoothly.

Note: try to see that *everyone* has a copy of this book, so that there is no 'mystique' or us-and-them divide involved.

UNIT 1
The Story

'The story that *must* be told!!!' screams the newspaper hoarding. Usually though, the reality is no more than the trivial scandal of a misspent, if well-paid, life! Some stories, however, really *do* have to be told – even at the cost of torture and death for the teller.

From the first Christian martyr, St Stephen, to those of today, exiled or imprisoned, there have been men and women in every generation who refused to be silenced. The story they told is ever the same. It centres on the life and work of one man, Jesus, the great Storyteller himself.

We, today, can hear their story. We may run the risk of being captivated by it. We face the challenge of having our lives changed by that story, and of finding ourselves compelled, through sheer joy, to tell that story ourselves.

It is human and right

– to ask questions about life and its meaning: the Greek philosopher Socrates said that 'the *unexamined* life is not worth living. Sooner or later we all ask deep within ourselves: What is life for? It is an important and sometimes painful question. But it is a question that must be asked.' (John Powell S.J., *Unconditional Love*)

– to stand in awe and wonder, or fear and rage, at the 'something' beyond us which we sense is 'there': 'How many men and women have looked up in fear at the thunder or the shadows in the forest and wondered about the power they sensed beyond the natural processes of the world and life?' (Ralph Martin, *Hungry for God*)

– to reconsider with an adult mind the simple answers given to us when children. 'If anyone has ears to hear, let him listen!' *Matthew 11:15*. What do we hear when we listen? We hear **stories**!

Stories take us *beyond* the world of simple **facts and figures**. All of the world's religions explain their deepest truths by means of stories. Stories can *stand for* more than that which is just touched and seen. The parables which Jesus told are such 'earthly stories with heavenly meanings'. Jesus did not invent this form of story – he was steeped in the Old Testament tradition which bursts with parables and allegories: the Creation stories, Jonah, Job and many others.

Whilst Jesus told stories about God's kingdom being close to the poor, the ordinary, the humble of heart – others were to tell stories about *him*. Matthew, Mark, Luke and John wrote their own collections of stories, which rang true to the memories of those who had heard and known Jesus. The Church continues to ensure that these stories, and their intended meanings, remain as authentic and true today as they were when told by those who knew Jesus, the Teacher from Nazareth.

At times in history it seemed that the interpretation which some people gave to the stories could have torn the Church apart. Each time such a 'heresy' threatened, the Church returned to the stories to discern, or seek out, the truth, with the guidance of God's Spirit of Truth. This would then be put into the form of a **statement of doctrine**. The Creed, said together at Sunday Mass, is a collection of such statements.

- **Stories** need discernment;
- **doctrine** helps us to interpret **stories** truly;
- there is no opposition between stories and doctrine.
- **Tradition** is made up of the **stories** and **doctrines** of the followers of Jesus throughout the years;
- **scripture** is part of the **tradition**;
- there is no opposition between scripture and doctrine.

Talking about God

When we talk about God in the form of **statements**, we can make some positive assertions:

God is all-knowing: 'Everything is uncovered and open to the eyes of [God].' *Hebrews 4:13*

God is almighty: '. . . nothing is impossible to God.' *Luke 1:37*

God is present everywhere: God is not bound by physical barriers, but is present to all and in all.

God is eternal: God is not bound by barriers of time, cannot be subject to ageing or decay. In God's time, all is present, all is NOW.

Greek philosophy helped us to make these statements about God. They help us to appreciate the 'Otherness' of God.

The Jews, the people of the Bible, so respect the 'Otherness' (or 'Transcendence') of God that they avoid using God's name (= 'Yahweh' = a form of 'I AM'), replacing it with 'The Lord', or a descriptive phrase. Being great storytellers, the Jews much prefer to describe *how* God works, rather than making statements. They describe God –

as a **potter**, moulding his creation: *Isaiah 64:8; Jeremiah 18:2ff;*

as a **warrior**, defending his people: *Exodus 15:1ff;*

as a **mother**, comforting her children: *Isaiah 66:13;*

as a **shepherd**, guiding his helpless sheep: *Psalm (22) 23.*

God's relationship with the community could be expressed in the language of the intimate love between a man and a woman. God's feeling for the people of Israel could be compared with the love a father has for his children and with the tenderness a mother feels for the child she nurses at the breast. (*Towards Adult Faith*)

Talking about ourselves: our story

When we begin to share the story of our lives with others, when we open up to our brothers and sisters, we can be helped to see how God is working in our lives. To hear the story of another's life and experience is to receive a precious gift. It is to discover an unwritten page of Scripture. We may need to develop the skill of attentive listening, and to pray for the discernment to be able to read God's story in another's life. For God is not *only* the Creator of worlds without end, the Sublime 'Otherness'; he also makes his home in all the many experiences of 'growing up, maturing, falling in love, settling down, working, recreating; in happiness, in sorrow, in health, in sickness, in success, in failure, in disappointment, in growing old, in dying.' (A. P. Purnell S.J., *Our Faith Story*)

Group Session

A word to the **Leaders** before the sessions start: For this first meeting it is important to establish the kind of atmosphere which such a course of sessions requires: warm, welcoming, friendly, confidential, non-pressuring, open, fun yet worthwhile.

In as comfortable and pleasant an environment as possible (if necessary, brighten up the room with posters, flowers, etc.), see that everyone is greeted on arrival, given a cup of tea or coffee, and seated in an arrangement in which all can see each other, rather than in stiff, formal rows. Music playing quietly in the background may help to break the ice. When all are settled and relaxed, the **Team Leader** can officially welcome everybody and introduce him/herself.

The Leader should also explain how the course is going to operate, and check that times and dates are convenient for most people (they never will be for all!). This is also a good time to find out if anyone will need lifts, babysitters or other practical assistance, and to put them in touch with someone who can help. Let each **Team Member** introduce him/herself, and just before breaking into groups of six to eight, have the **Session Leader** outline the **theme**. If participants have not yet had the opportunity to read the text for **Unit One**, it may be necessary to go through it in more detail than on future occasions when everyone will have read the text beforehand.

SMALL GROUPS

Get to know each other. Each person should briefly introduce him/herself – 'I'm Mary Mills, from the new estate by the hospital. I'm married to Jim, and have two boys, 8 and 13. I'm a housewife and a "lollipop lady". I've come with Jim, and know one or two people here.'

The next 'round' could involve a sharing of 'faith stories' and what members hope for from the course, e.g.
- 'I'm married to a Catholic, and would like to know more about it now the children are asking questions.'
- 'I was brought up a Catholic, but stopped going to church or anything, after First Communion. I'd like to know what it's really about now.'

Discussion could 'take off' from there, or may be helped by any of these questions:

- Have your ideas about Catholics or Catholicism changed over the years?
- How was the image or idea of God conveyed to you in the past? Which images have you found particularly helpful or unhelpful?
- Jesus was a great Storyteller. Which of the many stories Jesus told can you remember that helps you to imagine what God is like?
- Have you ever felt a real need for God in your life?
- How do you feel about the idea of God being interested and involved in every aspect of your life? Does it worry, comfort, or excite you? Can you believe it?

Has the Small Group any question or comment it would like to put to the full, large group and to the Team? It may be helpful to prepare one each Session.

After forty minutes, the groups could reassemble to form the Large Group.

LARGE GROUP

Invite introductions from all present, if numbers are not too great. Take any questions or comments from the Small Groups. Encourage everyone to read the text of the Unit to be used next, before the next meeting. Conclude with prayer.

PRAYER

For two or three minutes:

- be seated comfortably, hands relaxed, eyes closed;

- say over to yourself a word or phrase: e.g. 'Creator of the world', 'Jesus', 'Shepherd', 'Comforter'.
- allow an image of God to form in your mind;
- thank God for being the way God is, and for loving you.

When distractions occur, repeat the word you have chosen. Talk naturally, addressing God with your chosen word. Do not force the words. Be comfortable with silence.

After a suitable period, not too short to be rushed, nor too long to get boring, the Session Leader can introduce the concluding prayer, which could be one of the traditional prayers known to most Catholics. For this Session, the suggestion is that everyone should say together the *Glory Be*:

> Glory be to the Father,
> and to the Son,
> and to the Holy Spirit,
> as it was in the beginning,
> is now,
> and ever shall be
> world without end. Amen.

Seen in a parish magazine:

If there were no Creator, one scientist reflected, the odds against what has happened in creation are about the same as against a hurricane sweeping through a junk yard and leaving behind a Boeing 747 in perfect working order.

UNIT 2
The Journey

There is a view that treats 'faith' as if it were a 'thing'. You either have it or you don't! You can lose it, if you're not careful!

This view of faith tends to see God, not so much as a person, but as a 'Holy Being', or 'Thing', to be approached only by keeping a firm grip on the Faith-thing. Heaven help you if you ever mislay it or step out of line!

Let's change the picture – and look at faith rather as a living, growing relationship with God who is *active* in our changing lives. When St John wrote his Gospel, he did not once use the *noun* 'faith', but chose 98 times to use the *verb* form.

A noun is too static for John; the verb always indicates an active commitment – not faith but 'to believe in'. Thus 'to believe in' may be defined in terms of an active commitment to a person, and in particular, to Jesus. It involves much more than trust in Jesus or confidence in him, it is an acceptance of Jesus and of what he claims and a dedication of one's life to him.
(R. E. Brown, *The Gospel according to St John*, Vol I)

Our changing lives

In our lives as a whole, we are aware of much change and growth. We are not now as we were, not even as we were yesterday!

As **babies**, we absorbed – now we can reflect as well; as **children**, we accepted stories literally – now we can see meanings, interpret; as **adolescents**, unsure of ourselves, we conformed with others' expectations (maybe those of our rebellious friends!) – now, we can dare to be different, to think for ourselves.

Now, after a period of questioning which may have been long and challenging, we can accept ideas and meanings as our own. We can 'own' them for ourselves. Now, too, we know how far we have to *keep* growing. It is tempting to stay in the security of the past we know, rather than to take the risks that change might bring.

Yet there can be no growth without change: to become a flower, the seed must die. Growth in faith must involve taking risks. We cannot stand still.

I have not yet won, but I am still running, trying to capture the prize for which Christ Jesus captured me . . . I am racing for the finish . . . let us go forward on the road that brought us to where we are.
(*St Paul's letter to the Christians at Philippi, 3:12-16*)

Progress on the road of faith does not necessarily mean knowing lots of *facts* about God. The *faith-knowledge* of God is more like that between two lovers: spending time quietly together, yearning to be with the other and to love what the other loves.

Faith is the relationship, the incredible, tender love of God for me, and my tentative response. Beliefs describe the relationship: they attempt to put into words what faith is, so that I can share my faith with others.
(A. P. Purnell S.J., *Our Faith Story*)

God in our lives

We are all at different points along that road of faith. Each person has a unique, individual faith-journey. But we are not expected to make the journey on our own, unaided. The whole Church itself is a **people on the move**, a 'pilgrim people'. God is always actively with us, prompting each to help the other along the road.

When the Jews, our faith-ancestors, were enslaved in Egypt, and exiled to Babylon – when Jesus' own friends were caught up in his betrayal and execution – it seemed that misery, bondage and despair would always be their lot. It was only after liberation from these hardships that, on reflection, they could see that God had been *active* in their situations, always leading them along to freedom and fullness of life:

- from **slavery** in Egypt – through the desert to the Promised Land of Freedom;
- from **exile** in Babylon – to return with renewed ardour to Jerusalem;
- from **crucifixion** – to resurrection and new life for all.

God's own life = love in action

God is, and always has been, actively involved in human history, in the lives of each one of us. This follows from the very nature of God's own self. God *is* active relationship. This is expressed in terms of 'Trinity': Three Persons in the One God.

While the three Persons relate to each other and to us, as God's creation, God remains always One. There is only one God: one in nature, in substance and in essence; the beginning and the end of everything. It is the one God who revealed himself to Moses as the **I am** (*Exodus 3:13*) and to his people Israel as **The Lord** whom they were to love with all their heart and soul and might (*Deut. 6:4-5*). 'The mystery of the Most Holy Trinity is the central mystery of Christian faith and life. It is the mystery of God in himself. It is therefore the source of all the other mysteries of faith, the light that enlightens them.' (*Catechism of the Catholic Church*, 234)

The one God has been revealed as Father, Son and Holy Spirit:

God the Father is always, overflowingly, loving the Son, whom he brings into being (begets) every moment. This love knows no bounds, always exceeding everything that we can try to say or think about it.

God the Son responds with equally constant love. Jesus of Nazareth and the Son are one and the same, although for his earthly life, he 'did not count equality with God something to be grasped. But he emptied himself, taking the form of a slave, becoming as human beings are.' (*Philippians 2:6-7, New Jerusalem Bible version*)

God the Spirit, the 'Lord, the giver of life' (*The Creed*), is the Spirit of God's love. This immeasurable love expressed by Father to Son, Son to Father, is eternally bringing to life Creation's world to love and delight in. Life and love are one to God who is boundless, creative energy.

Group Session

LARGE GROUP

Welcome everyone; answer questions; review the theme. Prepare several voices to read the following passages concerning the Exodus experience:

> *Exodus 1:13-15*
> *Exodus 6:5-8*
> *Isaiah 41:10-14*
> *Exodus 15:1-2; 13:17-18*
> *Micah 6:4, 8*

Pick up and discuss any points of interest arising.

SMALL GROUPS
Ideas for discussion topics:

1. Looking back over our own faith-journeys, who has been the person who has most helped us along the way? Have there been others?

2. Has our journey been one of smooth, unwavering growth, or do any of the following diagrams say anything about our own experience?

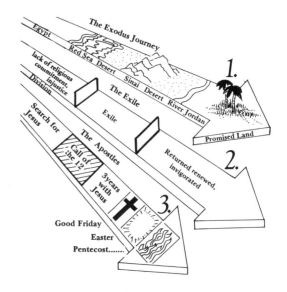

3. How does it help us to realise that we are *all* 'on the move' and at different points?

4. Have we ever experienced 'Exodus' in our own lives? Can we see where God has been actively liberating us? Do we feel we are still in bondage?

5. How might *we* describe what 'Faith' is? What 'Beliefs' are?

LARGE GROUP

Take any comments and questions from the groups. Are people feeling comfortable with the arrangements for these sessions? Are any changes requested?

Encourage everyone to spend some time at home in reading the text for the following session of whichever unit they all wish to explore next.

Lead into a short period of prayer by:

– ensuring the physical comfort of everyone (lights not too bright, no one in a draught, etc.);
– seeing that cups and plates are not being rattled, and that people are not moving about;
– allowing sufficient time (snatched moments well past the arranged 'closing time' are far from conducive to effective prayer!).

PRAYER

When all are calm and settled, breathing in a relaxed way, eyes closed, read *Luke 24:13-35* straight through. Then read it *slowly*, pausing as indicated, to ask the following questions (leave a moment of silence for the listeners to respond silently to these promptings):

1. *After verse 14:* we too have been sharing our stories; think back over the things which have been said, this Session and last. Be thankful for the gift of another's story.

2. *After verse 24:* the two disciples were open to the stranger. How open am I?

3. *After verse 27:* Christ uses Scripture to throw light on his story. How can I allow Scripture to shine its light on the experiences of my life, to see God's activity in the ordinary events of my story?

4. *After verse 28:* Christ does not force himself on others. Do I ever try to dominate, or force my opinions on others? Can I let people go, or do I cling on to them?

5. *After verse 29:* Am I so hospitable? So generous? – Thoughtful? – Welcoming?

6. *After verse 32:* does my heart burn within me as the Scriptures are explained? Do I recognise my Lord, Jesus the Christ, in the 'breaking of the bread'? At moments of great insight, am I aware of God's saving activity?

7. *After verse 35:* does reflection lead me to action? Do I find that I have to tell the story? *My* story? With whom shall I share my story?

Conclude by saying together the *Our Father* (in St Luke's Gospel)

> May your name be held holy,
> may your kingdom come.
> Give us each day our daily bread,
> and forgive us our sins as we forgive others,
> and deliver us from evil. Amen.

UNIT 3
Conversion

Karen tells her story

'I was a real tearaway by the time I was adopted. I'd gone through loads of foster-parents, making their lives hell! When I went to live with Mum and Dad just after I was eight, I didn't reckon I'd be with them for long. Every time I had a screaming fit, or whatever, I'd think "This is it! They'll send me back now, for sure." But they never did. I can't get over how patient they were with me. Over the years I changed, of course. I tried to be nicer to them. It didn't always work – but each time I'd turn back to them and know their love would be there. I only hope that when Trev and I marry and have kids, we'll be to them like my parents have been to me.'

Karen's conversion took years. There was no 'blinding flash' or instant emotional turn-about. To be a Christian means to experience 'conversion'. Maybe the lifelong process begins with a 'bang', a fundamental change of heart, or it begins almost unnoticed, from early childhood, little by little.

We are on a journey to God: we have not reached our goal. We are in the process of becoming: we have not yet become what we are called to be.
(A. P. Purnell S.J., *Our Faith Story*)

What *are* we called to be? We are called to be as fully *human* as was Jesus of Nazareth. He was a man who lived fully for God and for his brothers and sisters, all the world's people. He is God's answer to the question: 'What is *human*?'. How he is, is how God intends us to be.

Each time I make a choice for what is more fully human, I allow God's love to touch me and I respond to life. I yield a little selfishness, see a little clearer, trust a little more, so I journey on: God's love has worked a conversion (albeit very small) in me. Conversion is all about taking little steps towards becoming more and more human, according to God's understanding of human.
(A. P. Purnell S.J., *Our Faith Story*)

Religious conversion, the Canadian theologian Bernard Lonergan explains, is the basis for all others. Through this we learn to appreciate life as 'a mystery to be lived fully', a gift from God, rather than as an endless series of problems to be solved or obstacles to be overcome.

From this, we learn to accept and use our **emotions and feelings** creatively, seeing them as a normal part of human life. **Intellectually** we begin to let go of knowledge as just 'the facts' and see instead how knowledge can give **meaning** to our lives.

Finally, on the **moral** level, we need to be converted from making choices based either on 'the law' ('I'll get it in the neck if I don't . . .'), or on the selfish pleasure-principle. We learn how to apply the **values** we believe in.

God, not boot-straps!

Conversion is not something we can boast about: 'I pulled myself up by my boot-straps!' For *we* don't do the 'pulling up'; God does. On hearing the challenging words of Scripture, we may be provoked into responding to the invitation to be converted more closely into Jesus' image. But it is the ongoing presence of the Spirit in us, and in the encouragement others give us, which makes it possible. When '[Adults] hear the preaching of the mystery of Christ, the Holy Spirit opens their hearts, and they freely and knowingly seek the living God and enter the path of faith and conversion'. (*R.C.I.A. Introduction*, n. 1)

Even for those who knew Jesus intimately, the disciples, the path of conversion was long and rough: 'Gradually the initial yes that the disciples gave to Jesus deepened, was tested, failed and succeeded, and finally, after Pentecost, ripened into wholeheartedness.' (J. McKin, *Doorways to Christian Growth*)

Three conversion stories from Scripture

The blind man (*Mark 8:22-26*)

This man was brought to Jesus by his friends. Jesus led him gently by the hand out of the village, and in a quiet place, put spittle on his eyes and laid his healing hands upon him. Not that the man saw perfectly straight away; a second application was needed, and the point was made: perfect sight, full understanding, takes place in stages, gradually, just as the disciples only *gradually* came to grasp who Jesus really was.

Nicodemus (*John 3:1-21*)

Nicodemus, a leading intellectual in his day, disputed with Jesus, prompting him to expound some of his most significant teaching. Nicodemus' problem was that he could not go beyond the 'face value' of Jesus' words. He had to be patiently guided to go beyond their literal meaning. Later, Nicodemus was to defend Jesus against the hostile Pharisees (*7:50-51*).

A Samaritan woman (*John 4:4-42*)

A woman of dubious character, belonging to a people constantly at loggerheads with the Jews, this woman was to become an apostle, sent to preach the Good News to her own people! Such was her remarkable conversion. Like Nicodemus, she found it difficult to interpret Jesus' words. But when at length the truth dawned on her, she had to 'put down her water jar' and run to tell others. (The 'water jar' symbol of the Old Covenant is now replaced by the Living Water of the New, as it was with the Wine of the New at the Marriage Feast at Cana. (*John 2:1-10*))

The conversion of her people – the Samaritans – also occurred by stages: first, they heard about him from her; then they 'begged him to stay with them'. After two days of teaching from Jesus himself, they could *then* say: 'We have heard him ourselves, and we *know* that he really is the Saviour of the world.' (4:42)

Where may this conversion-process be taking us?

To be converted into the image of Jesus the Christ involves our behaviour, our life-style, our attitudes and our relationships. We need time and again, and deeper and deeper, to be liberated from our old ways and to take on newness in each area of life. The way we relate to God may need to be the first to change. We may have picked up some ideas of God which cannot be found in Scripture or the Tradition, and yet which vitally affect our relationship:

- we may see God as some form of impersonal Life-Force, or an old bearded man on a cloud;
- we may see Jesus as simply a 'Superstar', or as a stern Judge, sending down suffering on us as a 'punishment';
- we may see ourselves as having to merit or earn God's favour and mercy, and being generally unworthy and unlovable;
- we may see the Church as belonging to priests and bishops, who, unlike us, are by nature 'holy', and so forever telling us 'No, you can't!'

If we do, then conversion is called for, to help us:

• to relate to God as a fatherly, motherly, never-unloving Person;
• to relate to Jesus as the living risen Lord, healing now and liberating now, just as he served those he met in Palestine;
• to relate to the Holy Spirit as the power of the love of God, to be trusted and relied upon, rather than depend entirely on our own efforts and abilities;
• to relate to the Church as 'all of us', the whole Body of believers, both those alive now, and those who have gone before us, all holy, because all-loved by God.

Group Session

LARGE GROUP

Welcome everyone; answer questions; review the theme.

Consider: What does Scripture tell us that we need before there can be conversion? '. . . a heart to understand, eyes to see and ears to hear' (*Deuteronomy 29:3*, and many others). Jesus came '. . . so that those without sight may see' (*John 9:39*). Are we being called to see something new, or in a new way? Or, like the Pharisees, do we say 'We see'? (*John 9:41*)

Consider: *Ezekiel 36:25-28:* this is God's work. What can we expect might happen in our own lives? Do we welcome change and conversion? What might be the risks?

Consider: *Exodus 3:1-7:* what may have been 'burning bush' experiences in our lives?

SMALL GROUPS

At the moment when God was working through the great events of Scripture, people did not see him there. Afterwards, on reflection, they realised that God had been there, actively involved in their experience. This led them to praise and celebrate.

Suggestions for discussion topics: looking back on our own life experiences, can we recognise where God has been helping us to grow?

- How does Karen's story illustrate the theme of conversion?
- Have *you* a story to tell?
- Have any of your attitudes, views or opinions changed over the last ten, twenty or more years?
- What may have caused you to change your attitudes?
- What is meant by saying that 'conversion' is a life-long process?

LARGE GROUP

Deal with any comments or questions from the groups. Draw out the implication of seeing the following as *'either'*, *'or'*:

church as   (a) community,   *or*   (b) institution;

worship as   (a) celebration,   *or*   (b) duty;

faith as   (a) 'we . . .',   *or*   (b) 'I . . .';

authority as   (a) service,   *or*   (b) power.

– any others?

After discussion, lead into a time of prayer.

PRAYER

When all are still and relaxed, one (good) reader could read this poem, thoughtfully:

> Earth's crammed with Heaven,
> and every common bush afire with God;
> but only he who sees,
> takes off his shoes,
> the rest sit round it
> and pluck blackberries.

(Elizabeth Barrett Browning)

Allow time for the poem to 'work' in silence. If necessary, repeat it before concluding with everyone saying together this *Prayer of Abandonment* by Charles de Foucauld:

> Father,
> I abandon myself into your hands;
> do with me what you will.
> Whatever you may do, I thank you:
> I am ready for all, I accept all.
> Let only your will be done in me,
> and in all your creatures –
> I wish no more than this, O Lord.
> Into your hands I commend my soul;
> I offer it to you with all the love of my heart,
> for I love you, Lord, and so need to give myself,
> to surrend myself into your hands without reserve,
> and with boundless confidence,
> for you are my Father.

(from *Praise Him!*, edited by W. G. Storey)

UNIT 4
Jesus the Christ

If you ask a Christian 'What do you believe?', the answer you should get is 'Not what, but *who!*'

Christians believe above all *in* the person of Jesus Christ. Believing *in* means: giving all your trust, hope, whole life and being to a person, knowing that that person means more to you than anyone or anything else can. Catholics also believe (that is, accept as true) all that Jesus said and taught, as well as all that the Church says and teaches about Jesus. Many of the **sayings of Jesus** are stunningly challenging:

'Just as I have loved you, you must love one another. By this love . . . everyone will know that you are my disciples.' (*John 13:34-35*)

'To be a follower of mine . . . take up [your] cross daily and follow me . . . What gain is it . . . to have won the whole world and to have lost or ruined [your] very self?' (*Luke 9:23, 26*)

'If you forgive others their failings, your heavenly Father will forgive you yours.' (*Matthew 6:14*)

'If anyone wants to be first, he must make himself last of all and servant of all.' (*Mark 9:35*)

'Love your enemies, do good to those who hate you . . . pray for those who treat you badly.' (*Luke 6:27*)

'Alas for you [who] have neglected the weightier matters of the Law – justice, mercy, good faith!' (*Matthew 23:23*)

'Do not store up treasures for yourselves on earth . . . for where your treasure is, there will your heart be also.' (*Matthew 6:19-21*)

What effect do these sayings have?

- For many churchgoers, these sayings become rather too familiar and bland, and so lose their cutting edge.
- Some people can be turned off: those who see no need to change, whose life-styles are too comfortable to want to change (see too, *Mark 10:22*), or whose minds are closed (see *John 6:60*).
- Some Christians who really live these sayings find themselves the persecuted victims of oppressive regimes, for example in South America or the Far East.

Yet Jesus promised: 'If you make my word your home you will indeed be my disciples, you will learn the truth and the truth will make you free.' (*John 8:31-32*) Jesus sets his sisters and brothers free to *live* in the fullest way. He came: 'so that they may have life, and have it to the full'. (*John 10:10*)

With the fully lived life in mind, Christians choose not to prize too highly those values which come to an end when this life ends – such as success, power, wealth and good looks. Real achievements to be cherished would be:

- to have emptied yourself of all selfishness;
- to have laid down your life for others.

How the world would be transformed if there was real Christianity, where now so much lip-service is paid!

To know how to live this full life, Christians only have to look at the life of Jesus. Throughout the Gospels there shines out the picture of a man who cared passionately for people. He healed, he taught, he served, he gave himself for them to the last drop of his blood. To him all people were equally deserving of his love – the despised poor, women, tax-collectors, foreigners, the self-righteous and known sinners. To help them to find health, wholeness and joy, he showed them how to centre their attention and energy, not on themselves, but on the worship of God and the service of their fellow human beings. By giving them his love, he could move even the hardest hearts, as in this account of his encounter with an unpopular and crooked collector of taxes for the Romans: read *Luke 19:1-10*.

Pause for a moment:

- Is Jesus speaking to me as he did to Zacchaeus?
- How can I change my life, as Zacchaeus did his?

Why 'the Christ'?
(See *Luke 9:18-21*)

Of all the many titles and descriptions the Church gave to Jesus – Saviour, Redeemer, Shepherd, Lord – the Greek word 'Christ' (in Hebrew = 'Messiah') is the one given special importance. It means **Anointed One**. Anointing was associated in the Jewish world with the hope of healing and salvation. Also, priests, prophets and kings were anointed as a sign that they were to serve God and the people in a special way, with God's Spirit giving them the power to do so.

Throughout the long years when the Jewish people suffered under foreign rule, hope was mounting for a mighty military Messiah to arise and save them from oppression. Could Jesus of Nazareth, with his extraordinary gifts and large following, be the one? Imagine how confused and disappointed many were made to feel by his resolute non-violence, and especially by his cruelly humiliating death on a cross.

Victory

It took special, God-given, understanding by the disciples of Jesus to realise that in fact this agonising death really *was* the ultimate victory, and that the forces over which this victory had been won, sin and death, were far stronger and more powerful than the mighty Roman Empire.

The whole person (not just the body) of Jesus suffered on the cross, and the whole person (not just the soul) was raised from death to life. Christ, in a glorified body, is now wholly in heaven and yet with us too in a new way. No wonder that Christians celebrate that passing over from death to life as the central focus of all their worship.

The Easter event

This passing of Jesus from death to life with God the Father was proof that death itself had been conquered once and for all. In John's Gospel we are told how Jesus offers this same life-with-God to all people: 'I am the Resurrection and the life. If anyone believes in me, even though he dies he will live, and whoever lives and believes in me will never die. Do you believe this?' 'Yes Lord,' replied his friend Martha, 'I believe that you are the Christ, the Son of God, the One who was to come into the world.' (*John 11:25-27*) Martha expresses here the Christian understanding of 'Christ' – that he was the one who was able to share the very life of God with all who believe in him. Even death cannot blot out this sharing in the divine life, which is eternal as God is eternal, and in which 'your joy may be complete'. (*John 15:11*)

Group Session

LARGE GROUP

Welcome everyone; review the theme. Invite three or four team members to reflect briefly on prepared Gospel passages – those which provide special insights and value for them.

SMALL GROUPS

Each member takes a Gospel passage. When all have read and reflected, each reads out the chosen or given passage, then the Group discusses what it shows of Jesus and what it teaches us. Own choice, or select one of the following:

Mark 1:40-42 (*a healing*)
Luke 5:27-32 (*call of Levi*)
John 13:3-5; 12-15 (*serving*)
Mark 10:17-22 (*riches*)
John 4:5-10 (*Samaritan woman*)
Matthew 5:3-12 (*teaching*)
Mark 12:41-44 (*widow's mite*)
Luke 18:9-14 (*parable*)

Sharing in twos: Have you ever met anyone who seemed to bring you to life? What qualities did they have? Which values of Jesus do you personally find most difficult to live out?

LARGE GROUP

General discussion; deal with questions, etc. Encourage members to read the Introduction to the next Unit. Then create a prayer space and lead into . . .

PRAYER

Let everyone be quiet, relaxed, comfortable, breathing gently, with their eyes closed. The Leader says to all: 'Put yourself into the presence of our Lord, Jesus Christ. See him, hear him, praise him.

Then have a good reader read:
'In Thornton Wilder's play *Our Town*, a young woman dies and has the chance of re-living any one day from

her past. She chooses her tenth birthday, and sees it all again with the eyes now of experience, of reflection. She cannot go through with the whole day, the experience is too much for her, and she breaks down and "in a loud voice to the 'stage manager'" says: "I can't. I can't go on. It goes so fast. We don't have time to look at one another." (She breaks down, sobbing . . . and goes on): "I didn't realise. So all that was going on and we never noticed." After saying "good-bye" to all her childhood world, she adds: "Oh, earth, you're too wonderful for anybody to realise you." (She looks towards the stage manager and asks abruptly, through her tears) "Do any human beings ever realise life while they live it? – every, every minute?" The stage manager replies: "No . . . (pause), the saints and poets, maybe – they do some".'

Allow silence for the words of the play to 'work'. Then, if it seems to be necessary, the Leader says:

'Lord Jesus – lead us all to the fullness of life – to life which is realised every, every minute. Be with us, every, every minute. Open our eyes to the joy, the freshness, and wholeness of life – every, every minute.'
Conclude with everyone saying together:

1. Christ be beside me,
   Christ be before me,
   Christ be behind me,
   King of my heart.
   Christ be within me,
   Christ be below me,
   Christ be above me,
   never to part.

2. Christ on my right hand,
   Christ on my left hand,
   Christ all around me,
   shield in the strife.
   Christ in my sleeping,
   Christ in my sitting,
   Christ in my rising,
   light of my life.

3. Christ be in all hearts
   thinking about me,
   Christ be in all tongues
   telling of me.
   Christ be the vision
   in eyes that see me,
   in ears that hear me,
   Christ ever be.

(From *St Patrick's Breastplate*, adapted by James Quinn S.J.)

UNIT 5
Jesus and Us

Son of God

Jesus taught us to call God 'Our Father'. We are all the daughters and sons of God. Yet the relationship of Christ Jesus with the Father is unique: as the Christian Creed says, he is 'the only Son of God' and he 'came down from heaven for our salvation'.

Being the Word of God (*John 1*) communicated to us in human form, Jesus is everything that God wants to show us about God's own self. For in John's Gospel Jesus says, not just that – 'I have made known to you everything I have learnt from my Father' (*15:15*), but also: 'If you know me, you know my Father too.' (*14:7*)

Son of Man

This title, one that Jesus often used for himself, stresses the fact that he was human: that he had blood and bone and sinews. With a human mother, he grew up like any normal child of his time (what nonsense to say in a well-known carol: The little Lord Jesus, no crying he makes!). Of course he felt hunger, weariness, and at times anger. But above all he felt compassion. In him we find the true picture of real humanity: he was uniquely perfect. He was radically open to all people and to the will of his Father.

When Marie Blythe called at her daughter's one morning to visit her little grandchild, she found Ann in tears at the table, though the baby looked well and happy. 'Oh Mum,' she sobbed, 'have you seen the paper? And the news on the telly this morning? All that killing and violence! So much suffering and selfishness going on – what sort of a world is this to bring up Jason in?'

Marie knew what her daughter meant, and had sometimes asked herself the same question. The world can seem to be drowning in a flood of what can only be described as **sin**. We are all drawn into it, because we all live in the real world. The results of the sins of all of us are all around us – loneliness, despair, misery. Life really does not measure up to the advertisers' and the TV 'dream machine's' image. For many, it just falls apart in meaninglessness: a sudden bereavement or serious illness can force them to face the reality of their lives, and it can be frighteningly bleak.

There is nothing new here. Since the beginning of

human life it has been the same: only the technology has changed.

Sin-smashing!

What we need, desperately, is something to smash through the vicious cycle of violence and counter-violence, oppression-liberation-oppression, guilt and revenge. We might try, but our own efforts rarely *last* even when they do succeed. No power less than God's, the ultimate source of all reality, can do so.

As we see in Unit 4, God, through Jesus, has given us a brand-new start. As God alone can forgive sin, God the Son was sent to save and reconcile the whole world. The Christmas event, when God's son was born as a human baby, is linked inseparably with the Easter event, bringing together God's eternal time with our historic time. 'Only when the love of God for humanity becomes an event in history, can a new beginning be made in history.' (Walter Kasper, *Jesus the Christ*, Burns & Oates, 1976)

Solidarity

We now have a real alternative. Because this one person, Jesus, was perfectly obedient to God, totally loving, completely selfless and utterly sinless, he, human like us, could be intimately united with God. This allows each one of us to relate to God in a new way. No longer can we think of **God-up-there** and **us-down-here**. Because we all relate to Jesus Christ as our fellow human – all of us can share in the relationship with the Father which he enjoys supremely. Now, too, we can relate to each other in a new way, not as strangers but as sisters and brothers.

He has taken us out of the power of darkness and created a place for us in the kingdom of the Son that he loves, and in him we gain our freedom.
(*Colossians 1:13-14*)

We need not doubt the solidarity of Jesus with ourselves. He spoke of others *as if they were himself.*

Read:

- *Acts 9:4-5* (persecuted disciples = 'me')
- *Matthew 25:34-46* (to the least of my brothers = to me)

The Kingdom of God

'The time has come,' Jesus said, 'and the kingdom of God is close at hand. Repent, and believe the Good News.' (*Mark 1:15*)

The **Good News** is that the kingdom of God – the age of love – has begun in human history through the life, death and resurrection of Jesus Christ. It is a message of **joy**: all human hopes and longings can be fulfilled and a completely new start be made. All the old corrupt values are reversed: it is those who mourn, who are despised, poor, persecuted, the 'little' people, who are blessed!

It is a message of **life**: it refers to every act of God's will freely carried out in the 'here and now' by men and women. Every act of kindness, healing, forgiveness is a deed of both the 'doer' and of God. God invites us to have a share in his own life and to be God's partners in the on-going creation of the world.

It is a message of **hope**: as history is still going on, and all of us are still 'on the journey'. God's will is still in the process of being fulfilled, and so the kingdom is still 'coming'. We are assured that love *will* triumph over evil in the end, as it did at a point in history on a cross outside Jerusalem, and that the kingdom of God will arrive in its fullness. For this we pray daily: 'Thy kingdom come: thy will be done on earth as it is in heaven.'

Group Session

LARGE GROUP

Welcome everyone; answer questions. Review the theme: it may help you to draw out points by using *Titus 3:3-6*.

SMALL GROUPS

Examine the following statements about Jesus. Circle the 'yes' or 'no' after each, then discuss results, spending time on the apparently difficult areas of Christology.

Is it true that Jesus –

- was a good man, but little more than that? yes/no
- was God, just seeming to be human? yes/no
- was a circumcised Jew? yes/no
- knew everything about everything from infancy? yes/no
- was not able to sin? yes/no
- is related to all of us? yes/no
- offers us a life of pleasure? yes/no
- prefers some people to others? yes/no
- affects our lives only after death? yes/no
- performed miracles as signs that God's kingdom had come? yes/no
- rewards only those who have deserved it? yes/no
- is living, loving and active now? yes/no

In twos: if you had to describe Jesus to a Martian, what would you choose to say about him? Write down your ideas in just one or two sentences, then tell your partner. Explain any words which a Martian with poor English would find difficult!

LARGE GROUP

General discussion. Leader to witness what Jesus means to her/him. If there is time, invite others to tell who Jesus is for them. Move into time for prayer.

PRAYER

When ready, invite everyone to repeat, phrase by phrase, the *Jesus Prayer*:

> Lord Jesus Christ,
> Son of the Living God,
> have mercy on me, a sinner.

Then, in silence, invite everyone to repeat that phrase over and over . . . letting it sink deep into the heart . . . slowly, with meaning . . . (silence).

At the end of a suitable period of, it is hoped, *active* prayer, conclude with everyone saying the *Compline Prayer*:

Save us, Lord, while we are awake;
protect us while we sleep;
that we may keep watch with Christ
and rest with him in peace. Amen.

UNIT 6
Scripture:
Old Testament

'At various times in the past and in various different ways, God spoke to our ancestors.' *Hebrews 1:1*

Jews and Christians share much in common. The Good News of God's love for all people was first revealed to the Jews, the people chosen by God for a purpose. To be the Chosen People meant that they were to be the **sign of God's love** for all people. It was during their long history that this Sign became perfected in one of their number, Jesus. Since then both Christianity and Judaism have upheld the values and cherished the revealed insights of who God is, found in the books of the Hebrew Bible (Old Testament).

Who wrote the books of the Old Testament?

At the deepest level, God is the author of the Scriptures. God is speaking to us throughout the written words of people. Those who wrote down or edited all the stories, poems and accounts (some of which were already many hundreds of years old) naturally used their own understanding and style. Remember that people of other ages and countries use language differently from the way we do today. For example, in the early stages of history, to show that some people led good lives, blessed by God, their ages were highly exaggerated: Kenan lived for 905 years and Methuselah for 969!

If you are bothered by some accounts which do not tally with the discoveries of modern science, look instead for what the author *meant* by the story. What is intended is probably a **parable-story** – at one level about ordinary life, but at a deeper level about God and heavenly matters. The deeper level is the important one.

Genesis, the 'Book of Beginnings' contains many of these 'parables'. Through them we can learn that the Creator-God made human beings in his own image, both men and women equally, and gave them **free will** – freely to accept or freely to reject God's love. We can see that by rejecting God's love and disobeying his loving commands, sin with its consequences is let loose in the world. Yet God is shown as never giving up on his creation. To the obedient **Noah** 'and every living thing that is found on the earth' (*Genesis 9:17*) God offered a Covenant (i.e. a relationship based on promises) marked with the sign here of a rainbow.

Abraham too, our 'father in faith' was offered a Covenant with the promise of his people becoming a nation under God's special care. Shedding the blood of sacrificial lambs was to be offered as *an act of worship, appeal for forgiveness*, and as a means of *renewing* the nation's relationship with God. Circumcision was required of the male population as the sign that the Covenant was endorsed by the people. Abraham's grandson **Jacob** (also called 'Israel') had twelve sons who each founded a tribe which together became the nation of Israel. One of these sons, Joseph, helped the people to settle in Egypt, where they eventually became slaves of the Pharaoh, and were forced to labour in the building of the pyramids and palaces.

Three key points of Old Testament History

1. **Moses** led Israel from slavery in Egypt through the Red Sea to a new life. A new Covenant (see *Exodus 19*) was made between God and the people, based on the Ten Commandments and the Teaching, or **Law** (in Hebrew = Torah). (The Torah was eventually either written down, especially in the first Five Books of the Bible, or passed on in spoken traditions, which developed as time passed.) After Moses, the people settled in Canaan (which the Romans later called 'Palestine' after the Philistine people). They became first farmers, then town-dwelling crafts- and tradespeople.

   Tribal organisation tends to break down when people begin to live in towns. Old loyalties give way to new, and people need to find security and pride in different social structures. For the Jewish people at this time, the sense of being part of a united and great nation was given popular expression with the appointment of the first national king, Saul.

2. **David** was the second king, and proved to be a brilliant politician. He established Jerusalem as the military and political centre of a powerful nation. He built the First Temple, later made magnificent by his

son, **Solomon**, making it the centre of all religious life and worship. After Solomon, the kingdom split into two rival kingdoms: North = Israel, and South = Judah (from which comes the word 'Jew'). Mighty empires were rising in the East. First Assyria swallowed up Israel in 722, and then the Babylonian Empire took Judah, forcing many of her inhabitants into Exile in Babylon in 586 B.C.

3. **Exile**. During these painful years, urged by prophets, some (a 'remnant') stayed faithful to God and the Torah, and began to hope for a Messiah to restore to them the glory of David's reign. They did return, and rebuilt the devastated Temple, but were ruled over by foreign powers – Persian, then Greek and finally Roman. The Romans destroyed Jerusalem in A.D. 70 and sent the Jewish people out throughout the world. Since then, whether in Spain, Eastern Europe, the U.S.A. or, since 1948, Israel again, the Jews have kept and developed their deep faith in the One God and still keep as many of their ancient traditions as they can.

The Hebrew Bible (Old Testament)

The Hebrew Bible was divided by the Jews into *three* sections:

1. Teaching (Torah)

Genesis, Exodus, Leviticus, Numbers, Deuteronomy

The whole Bible teaches about God, but these first five books 'of Moses' are specially sacred. They contain pre-history parable-stories, the origins of Jewish history and religion, and the rules for conducting a God-centred society.

2. The Prophets

The 'Earlier' Prophets
Joshua, Judges, Samuel (I & II), Kings (I & II)

The 'Later' Prophets
Isaiah, Jeremiah, Ezekiel
The Twelve (Hosea, Joel, Amos, Obadiah, Jonah, Micah, Nahum, Habakkuk, Zephaniah, Haggai, Zechariah, Malachi)

Christians classify some of these as books of 'history', whereas in Jewish tradition emphasis is put on their 'prophetic' value – speaking of God's truth to people of all times.

The task of the prophets is to call the people back to true religion. 'What does the Lord require of you but to do justice, and to love kindness, and to walk humbly with your God?' (*Micah 6:8, Revised Standard Version*)

Through them, God reveals his promise of the Age of Christ ('Messianic Era') expressed with stunningly poetic beauty in *Isaiah 40-55* (highly recommended reading!).

3. The Writings

Psalms, Job, Proverbs, Ruth, Song of Songs, Ecclesiastes, Lamentations, Esther, Daniel, Ezra-Nehemiah, Chronicles

These books involve the response of people to God's revelation, particularly in the Teaching.

The Greek Bible

This is a Greek translation of all the Hebrew books above, plus seven later books written in Greek: Tobit, Judith, Maccabees I & II, Wisdom, Ecclesiasticus, Baruch – and parts of Esther and Daniel.

All forty-six of these were in use by, and accepted by, the Christian Church by the year A.D. 100. They have continued to be the books of the Catholic and Orthodox Bibles. The sixteenth-century Reformers accepted only the thirty-nine Hebrew books. Now though, through 'joint' Bibles and Bible Study, many accept and value those books once called **Apocrypha** (= hidden). In the early days of the Church, there were many 'apocryphal' books in circulation, but the Church was guided by the Holy spirit to select only those which are sound in teaching and true in revelation.

When was the Old Testament written?

For hundreds of years stories, songs and prayers were passed on by word of mouth. It is not easy to date when they *started* to be written down. Certainly not before reading and writing had begun to be more widely used, about 900 B.C., with most books being written or assembled over several centuries. The Torah was finished and accepted by 400 B.C. and the Prophets by the second century B.C. The youngest of all the books, Wisdom, was probably complete by 50 B.C.

Group Session

LARGE GROUP

Welcome everyone; answer questions; review the theme. It may be necessary to expand on 'Covenant', 'Torah', or symbolic *versus* literal language.

Three or four team members could share a passage from the Old Testament that is considered significant. Any impression that the God of the Old Testament is vengeful or savage, unloving or remote should be discussed and corrected.

SMALL GROUPS

Members could share their own favourite passage, or spend three or four minutes on each of the following:

Ezekiel 37:21-28 (*promise of the age of the Messiah*)
Isaiah 55:3-9 (*promise of a New Covenant*)
Deuteronomy 24:14-22 (*justice*)
Isaiah 61: 1-2 (see also Luke 4:18) (*Good News*)
Joel 2:12-13 (*call to real repentance*)
Psalm 89:1-4 (*hymn to God's faithfulness*)
Isaiah 49:13-16 (*God never abandons his people*)
Exodus 19:3-8 (*obedience demanded and accepted*)

Pray together – based on the meditative use of **Psalms**, possibly *no. 23, no. 24,* and/or *no. 139* (omit *verses 19-22!*).

LARGE GROUP

Deal with any comments or questions from the groups. Invite people to share what seemed to them strikingly insightful or helpful, then create a prayerful atmosphere.

PRAYER

Invite members to look at *Psalm 27* (Yahweh is my light and my salvation) in the *Jerusalem Bible* version, if possible. If not everyone has a copy, have it read aloud, slowly and carefully. Then ask members to ponder the phrases which seem to be relevant to their own lives and faith-stories; let the phrases work within each person; how do members *feel* at this moment?

Conclude with everyone saying together the *Prayer of St Francis*:

> Lord, make me an instrument of your peace:
> where there is hatred, let me sow love;
> where there is injury, pardon;
> where there is doubt, faith;
> where there is despair, hope;
> where there is darkness, light;
> and where there is sadness, joy.
>
> O Divine Master,
> grant that I may not so much seek
> to be consoled as to console,
> to be understood as to understand,
> to be loved as to love.
>
> For it is in giving that we receive;
> it is in pardoning that we are pardoned,
> and it is in dying that we are born to
> eternal life.

UNIT 7
Scripture:
New Testament

'More blessed still are those who hear the word of God and keep it!' (*Luke 11:28, New Jerusalem Bible version*)

Whenever St Francis found a scrap of paper lying beside the road, he would lift it carefully and bear it away with great reverence – just in case written on it were words of God from a Bible.

What a shock he would find in today's world! We are bombarded daily by words of all sorts – written and spoken, processed and programmed! How hard it is for us to recognise the few that give life from all the rest. And yet 'What food, what honey could be sweeter than . . . to look into the mind of the Creator, to listen to the Lord's words?' – as the fourth-century Bible scholar St Jerome wrote to Paula, a Roman lady who had learned the whole Bible by heart!

My one desire for all the Church's children [is] that, being saturated with the Bible, they may arrive at that all-surpassing knowledge of Jesus Christ.
(Pope Benedict XV, *Spiritus Paraclitus* encyclical, 1920)

Jesus himself is the 'Word made flesh' (*John 1*). God speaks to us in him, through his life and his words. 'When your words came, I devoured them. Your word was my delight and the joy of my heart.' (*Jeremiah 15:16*)

God reveals himself through all the words of Scripture. The words themselves may not at first convey much to us. We all need help to discover in them fully the Good News that the authors intended. Like the chief treasurer of Ethiopia in the account in *Acts 8:26-40*, when asked if he understood the prophet Isaiah whom he was reading, we too answer: 'How can I unless I have someone to guide me?'

Over the centuries there have been very many Christians, especially of the Reformed traditions, who have felt themselves to be individually guided by the Holy Spirit alone. Their great practice of reading the Bible privately has been of enormous help in nurturing and sustaining the faith of generations. Yet individual guidance needs to be tested with the mind of Christ, and who can guide with the mind of Christ if not the Body of Christ, the Church? (See Unit 8 for a fuller explanation of the 'Body of Christ'.) As the Bible is the collection written by the Church, to explain what the Church believes, naturally it should be the Church which can best explain it to us. The disciples on the road to Emmaus felt their 'hearts burning within' them as the Risen Christ explained the Scriptures to them (*Luke 24:32*). The Chief Ethiopian Treasurer was converted and baptised after Philip, starting from a Bible text, explained the Good News of Jesus to him. So today, lives are changed when people hear the Good News authentically presented to them.

The force and the power in the word of God is so great that it remains the support and energy of the Church, the strength of faith for her sons, food for the soul and the pure and perennial source of spiritual life.
(*Decree on Revelation*, n. 21, Vatican II)

Scripture in Church

At the celebration of every Mass, the Church proclaims the word of God in readings, teaching (homily) and prayers. Indeed Scripture (Liturgy of the Word) has always been venerated by the Church which has considered the Liturgy of the Word and the Liturgy of the Eucharist to form together one single act of worship. 'She never ceases to present to the faithful the bread of life, taken from the one table of God's Word and Christ's Body.' (*Decree on Revelation*, n. 21)

It is good to read in advance the portions of Scripture to be used at Mass, and to listen attentively when they are read, for 'Christ himself is present in His word since it is He Himself who speaks when the Holy Scriptures are read in Church.' (*Constitution of the Liturgy*, n. 7, Vatican II) 'To ignore Scripture is to ignore Christ.' (*Pope Benedict XV, after St Jerome*)

How do we read or hear the Word of God?

- With **prayer**: with an attentive, prayerful attitude, like that of young Samuel in the Temple; 'Speak, Lord, your servant is listening.' (*1 Samuel 3:10*)
- With **reflection**: considering how our own life or experience is being addressed by these words.
- With **action**: if action does not follow, we are simply being entertained. 'People with a noble and generous heart . . . hear the word of God and put it into practice.' (*Luke 8:15, 21*)

How the New Testament came into being

The books of the Old Testament, which were the Scriptures for Jesus and the early Church, contained much that had been used for worship before being written and collected. In the same way material which made up the New Testament was preached, taught and believed by the People of God before any of it was collected together as Scripture. There was much more written than that which was finally selected, but the Church included as Holy Scripture only what it considered authentic.

- First is **Jesus** – preaching the Good News (= Gospel) of the Kingdom of God. All that Jesus says and does is Gospel, which he passes on to his apostles, or special 'envoys'.
- Then these **apostles**, the first Bishops of the Church, 'preach every day both in the Temple and in private houses . . . their proclamation of the Good News of Christ Jesus'. (*Acts 5:42*) Through these people, and their descendants, the Church grows, with new communities springing up throughout the Eastern Mediterranean.
- Finally, **writing** is necessary – to send letters off to the new communities to follow up infrequent visits. Thirteen of these by St Paul, and eight others, are found in the New Testament. The first one, to the new group of Christians at Thessalonika, was probably written more than 20 years after Jesus told his followers to 'Go, make disciples of all the nations'. (*Matthew 28:19*)

Four versions of the Gospel

While the apostles were still living, with their memories fresh, it was enough to convey the Gospel by speech. The time arrived when it became necessary to write down accounts of 'everything that Jesus had done and taught' (*Acts 1:1*), although really 'there were many other things that Jesus did; if all were written down, the world itself, I suppose, would not hold all the books that would have to be written'. (*John 21:25*) So, the writers had to edit and select, to choose those sayings and anecdotes of Jesus from the current collections, and, under the inspiration of the Holy Spirit, to set down their accounts to reflect the Church's teaching and to meet the religious needs of their intended readership/audience.

None of the four writers, or Evangelists (= 'messengers of Good News') intended to write a simple 'biography' of Jesus, nor did they know their version of the Gospel would be included one day in 'Scripture'. They just wrote the truth which they and their community believed, in their own words, and for one purpose: 'so that you may believe that Jesus is the Christ, the Son of God, and that believing this you may have life through his name'. (*John 20:31*)

Tradition has passed down to us the names and backgrounds of the Evangelists and the sequence of the Gospels, but none of these claims is established definitively. Scholars are constantly in the process of shedding new light on these matters and discovering fresh insights into the communities of early Christians which produced these Gospels.

St Mark, possibly St Peter's secretary and interpreter, wrote after St Peter's death, about A.D. 65 to encourage the persecuted Christians in the Rome of Nero.

St Matthew, one of the twelve apostles, after the destruction of Jerusalem in A.D. 70, wrote for Jews and Jewish Christians, emphasising that Jesus is the Messiah, the new Moses. Even in his first sentence, he links Jesus with both David and Abraham, key figures of Jewish faith.

St Luke, like St Matthew, used a lot of material from St Mark's version. Luke was a Greek-speaking Gentile, and possibly secretary to St Paul. He wanted all people to believe in Jesus. In his version of Jesus' family-tree, he links Jesus with both David, and Adam, first 'parent' of all people.

St John's version of the Good News was written possibly as late as A.D. 100 or so. This version is strikingly different from the other three, based as it is on teaching illustrated by seven 'signs' (miracles), and prayers, speeches and deeds of Jesus not mentioned in the other Gospels. Jesus is seen here strongly representing the fulfilment of the Law, Old Testament prophecy and the themes of the Festivals.

Links with the Old Testament

Much New Testament literature reflects the Christian interpretation of the Old Testament. One early Christian tradition is of seeing various Old Testament people and events as 'types', or 'foreshadowings' of those in the New who are their counterparts. Jesus is seen in very many ways as fulfilling Old Testament 'types', some of which are:

Jesus as:
- the new and perfect **Adam**, making up for his disobedience by perfect obedience;
- the new **Moses**, leading us to the Promised Land of Eternal Life;
- the new **David**, as Messiah-King whose rule is Perfect Love;
- the **Suffering Servant** in the book of Isaiah 'and through his wounds we are healed' (*Isaiah 53:5*);
- the new **Temple**, 'destroy this sanctuary and in three days I will raise it up' (*John 2:19*), through whom is perfect worship 'in Spirit and in truth' (*John 4:23*), and who is both priest and victim.

Group Session

LARGE GROUP

Welcome everyone; answer questions. Give instructions for the Small Group session, to allow each group to choose its 'target audience'.

Each group is to compose a short account of the Good News, selecting and moulding the material appropriately, so that it makes sense to, and influences, one of these:

a) a highly religious non-Christian group;
b) a bored, uncaring teenage group;
c) a group of young children;
d) a group of torturers and death-squad 'hit-men';
e) any other?

SMALL GROUPS

Each group to select its 'target audience', and then to spend ten minutes discussing their ideas; allow five minutes for someone to write down the account, and five minutes for finishing off. Return to the Large Group.

LARGE GROUP

One member from each Small Group should read the results of their labours. Then everyone can discuss the accounts and compare them with the Gospels.

Move then into a discussion of recent readings at Mass, if any can be recalled! What stood out as memorable, striking, puzzling, challenging, etc.? Invite one or two **Readers** to share how they prepare each reading, and what structures there are in the lectionary. Display materials which give insights into the readings, such as 'Preaching and Teaching the Word' in *Priests & People*, *Scripture Bulletin* and *Focus the Word*. Show Bible commentaries, such as *The New Jerome Biblical Commentary* and versions of Bibles which give good notes. The best are the 'Standard' or 'Study' versions of the *Jerusalem Bible* or the *New Revised Standard Version*. Answer or note questions and deal with any practical matters then move into a time of prayer.

PRAYER

Invite people to read quietly, or have read to them, *Philippians 2:1-11*. Allow the words to speak directly to you.

Consider: 'These words were written *to* me; these words were written *about* me.' Just 'ruminate' on the words. Go over them, digest them slowly.

After a time, conclude with everyone saying together:

> Thank you, Lord Jesus Christ,
> for all the benefits and blessings
> which you have given me,
> for all the pains and insults
> which you have borne for me.
> Merciful Friend, Brother and Redeemer,
> may I know you more clearly,
> love you more dearly,
> and follow you more nearly,
> day by day.

(St Richard of Chichester)

UNIT 8
The Holy Spirit and the Church

Why should men love the Church? Why should they love her laws?
She tells them of Life and Death, and of all that they would forget.
She is tender where they would be hard, and hard where they like to be soft.
She tells them Evil and Sin, and other unpleasant facts.
They constantly try to escape
from the darkness outside and within
by dreaming of systems so perfect that no one will need to be good.
But the man that is will shadow
the man that pretends to be.
(from *The Rock*, by T. S. Eliot)

'No man is an island' – we readily agree with John Donne. We know how dependent we all are on each other – for food, fuel, clothes, language, knowledge – and so much more. We were created for relationships, for belonging, for giving. We may be most aware of this through the pain of broken relationships or loneliness. The perfect relationship of love is that of the 'private life' of God, in whose image we were created – the family of the Trinity: Father, Son and Holy Spirit (see Unit 2). Such love as theirs, so limitless and generous, is available for all to share. For when Jesus was about to leave his disciples, he promised them that he would not leave them orphans, but would send the **Paraclete** (= helper) – the Holy Spirit – to be with them for ever. Jesus had to leave the confines of time and space (first-century Palestine) in order to be with all people everywhere. In the Spirit, Jesus is no less present to contemporary disciples than he was to those with whom he walked beside the lake of Galilee.

This same Creator-Spirit who had formed the world and the human race (read *Genesis 1*) was to form a **new creation**: a People, from every race, class and age, united in faith and love, to work as partners with the

Christ, who had been sent: 'not to condemn the world, but so that through him the world might be saved'. (*John 3:17*)

The Spirit came (and how!) to the apostles, Jesus' mother and a few other men and women followers on the **Festival of Pentecost**, recorded in *Acts 2*. From among the first Chosen People of Israel, this handful of disciples formed the beginning of a Catholic (= world-wide) Church which was to proclaim the Good News of Christ Jesus across the centuries. On that Pentecost, the prophecy of Joel had begun to be fulfilled: '(It is the Lord who speaks) – I will pour out my Spirit on all humanity . . . (and) all who call on the name of the Lord will be saved.' (*Acts 2:17, 21, New Jerusalem Bible version*) The Spirit is poured out freely on all, enabling people to resist the pressures of selfishness and sin, and to draw towards the light of Truth. By **baptism**, this gift is celebrated and accepted. From that time, all the gifts and talents which God has given will be used for his service. The first step to full participation in the Christian Church is taken and the start of a new life lived in relationship with fellow-Christians made.

Through the Church's Tradition – the handing down through history of the word of God and the sacraments – we not only learn of, and worship, God, but also actually encounter God in many real and intimate ways. In the Eucharist particularly, each participant is in the closest possible union with both God and fellow Christians. The community then is *fully* 'the Church'.

The Christian Church is the context within which each of its members continues to fulfil God's work of creation and salvation. While it may have elements of the following, the Church is *not* a social club, a 'holy huddle' or a bossily led Institution. It *is* all of the following descriptions, and infinitely more besides:

• People of the New Covenant
Jeremiah was promised (*31:31, 33*) that one day God 'will make a new Covenant with the House of Israel . . . Deep within them I will plant my Law, writing it in their hearts. Then I will be their God and they shall be my people.' This was sealed on behalf of both God and

people by the blood Jesus shed on the cross, to which he referred during his Last Supper (see *Luke 22:20*).

• **The Body of Christ**

Through the Spirit, Christ unites his followers into a living body, his Body – with Christ as the head. As all the parts of a human body together form one body, so each member of the Church, with her or his special gifts and talents given by the Spirit, is united to the Body of Christ – the Church.

• **The meeting-place of God and People**

It is in the Church that people can fully be what they were intended to be: in touch with the world and in touch with God; reaching out to others, reaching up to heaven.

The Church is the centre upon which all lives converge, in order that the creatures of the one God may not live as strangers or enemies one with another, having no place in common, where they may display their love and their peace.
(Maximus the Confessor)

The Church and the world

The Church is not a group of 'holier-than-thou' people set apart from the world. All Christian people are very much *in* the world and *for* the world – and yet, for Christians there is more to life than just the values, goals and achievements *of* this world. They are responding to the truly human need to reach beyond; they live in the knowledge that death is not the end of everything.

Their lives are constantly unsettled by the probing challenge of the Gospel, yet their happiness lies precisely in following that demanding call to walk in the steps of Christ.

The misery of our race is a result of a persistent quest for happiness in the wrong places.
(H. Chadwick, on St Augustine, *Tablet* 24/5/86)

That is why, until the whole world shares this lasting happiness, the Christian Church is 'a pilgrim Church. This Church is not an army marching in formation, but more like a group of travellers in a desert . . . and for most it is a journey of hope and expectation' (p. 11 from Summary of Consultation *Called to Serve* for Synod '87). During the journey the Christian is called to help to bring life to that desert, the world. The Church, as the living Body of Christ in the world, has been entrusted with the world.

Christ has no body now on earth but yours; no hands but yours; no feet but yours; yours are the eyes through which Christ looks with compassion on the world; yours are the feet through which he is to go about doing good; yours are the hands with which he is to bless men now.
(St Teresa of Avila)

Entrusting the world to human beings, even with the help of the Spirit and the Church, was certainly a risk for God to take. We all know, painfully, the gap there is between what *is* and what *should be*. Even the story of the Church itself (see Unit 9) is not without its horrors and failings. We do not have to be in a parish long to be aware of many causes for grumbling and complaints! Yet, despite all the faults – the sins within us and in the Church and the world, Christ entrusts the world to us still.

There is no greater dignity or challenge than to know that one is trusted by God, with all one's weaknesses and strengths, one's limitations and gifts. Since Christ has entrusted his Church to all of us, to live and preach his gospel of justice, love and peace, we are called to deepen our own trust in his Spirit and in each other.
(*Easter People*, n. 16)

Christians, divided yet one

So far, *one* Christian Church has been mentioned – formed by Christ through the Holy Spirit by means of the apostles: they who had heard the Good News from Jesus himself, spread it and passed it on, sharing their mission with others. Within a short time missionaries were being sent out from the twin Imperial centres of Constantinople and Rome. Those from Constantinople had developed their own patterns of prayer and Eucharist, and their particular customs, including their own date for Easter. Some of the Churches which they founded broke with the Church of Rome in the eleventh century. These are called the **Orthodox Churches**. A small number have since returned to Full Communion with the Bishop of Rome, the Pope.

The **Catholic Church** includes those of the **Roman (Latin or Western) Rite**, as well as those of about a dozen **Oriental Rites** (e.g. Byzantine, Coptic, Maronite, Ukrainian, etc.).

From one point of view the Roman Rite (Roman Catholic) Church can be seen as a federation of local area Churches whose bishops are in Full Communion with each other and with the Bishop of Rome. From another, it is perceived very much as a single unit.

Christians in the West were divided at the time of the Reformation (sixteenth century), and whilst a large number continued in the Catholic Church, many others could not accept the whole tradition of Scripture, faith and sacraments in the forms in which the Catholic Church handed them down. These broke away to form the **Protestant** or **Reformed Churches**, which developed their own traditions according to the different emphases of their founders or leading members. Rather different in origin is the Anglican Communion, whose varied practices and wide range of doctrinal positions helps it to span the gap between the Reformed and the Catholic traditions (see also Unit 19).

The (Catholic) Church knows that she is joined in many ways to the baptised who are honoured with the name of Christian, but who do not however profess the Catholic faith in its entirety or have not preserved unity or communion under the successor of (St) Peter (= the Pope) . . . these Christians are indeed in some real way joined to us in the Holy Spirit for, by his gifts and graces, his sanctifying power is also active in them.
(Constitution on *The Church*, n. 15, Vatican II)

To unite all the Christian Churches into one undivided communion is the urgent desire of many of Christ's followers from all traditions, so that the prayer of Jesus may be fulfilled: 'that they may be so completely one that the world will realise that it was you (Father) who sent me and that I have loved them as much as you loved me' (*John 17:23*). (See also Unit 19.)

Mary, Mother of God

Catholics have always held Jesus' mother, Mary, in high esteem, honouring her with a number of titles – particularly **Our Lady**, and **Blessed Virgin**. She is remembered affectionately as the one who, with her husband Joseph, provided the child Jesus with a human model of love and wisdom – steeped as she was in the pious traditions of her Jewish heritage. She was present at Jesus' first public miracle, at the wedding feast at Cana, and at her son's cruel death. She was prominent at the descent of the Holy Spirit on the apostles at Pentecost and, Catholics believe, is still close to her son in heaven, joining and strengthening our prayers with her own.

The reasons for her pre-eminence in the Church are many. Her response to the Angel Gabriel when the word of God was announced to her has become a model for all Christians. She not only heard the word – and was the first to hear the Gospel, or Good News, concerning Jesus, the Son of God and inheritor of God's promises to David (*Luke 1:32-33*) – she also accepted it in faith and acted upon it: she went at once to share the Good News with another, her relative Elizabeth. Hearing, accepting and acting on the word of God is the mark of the true disciple as Jesus shows in *Luke 8:4-21*. Here the parable of the sower is illustrated by the example of Jesus' mother and brothers (= close relatives) as those who 'hear the word of God and put it into practice'.

In Mary's praise of God: the **Magnificat**, recorded in *Luke 1:46-55* (see page 73), the later Gospel message of the *Beatitudes* (6:20-26) finds joyful expression. So Mary both accepts and proclaims the Gospel, representing in herself the honour God gives to those who are powerless and weak in the world's eyes.

When Jesus was dying on the cross, John's Gospel reports that he offered the 'beloved disciple', John, to be to her as a son, and for her to be a mother to John. The term used – 'woman' – suggests something deeper than is apparent: that Mary, the new Eve (Woman) was to be the spiritual mother of the whole Church, represented by John. Mother of Jesus, Lord and brother to us all; Mother of the Church; model disciple. Whenever Mary is remembered and invoked, God's generosity and graciousness are brought to mind. The influence of Mary on people 'does not hinder in any way the immediate union of the faithful with Christ but on the contrary fosters it'. (*The Church*, n. 60, Vatican II)

Group Session

LARGE GROUP

Welcome everyone; answer questions. Explore the theme of Pentecost – the way in which the apostles changed from fear to bold proclamation of the Gospel. Discuss the effect of the Holy Spirit on people in

Scripture and in the Church. Encourage personal testimony by members of the parish, prayer groups, etc.

Discuss which of many of the models of the Church are found most helpful; some examples:

- Divine Institution
- Pilgrim People
- Barque of Peter
- Vine
- Servant of God
- Body of Christ
- Sheepfold
- Rock
- any others?

SMALL GROUPS

Suggested topics for discussion:

1. What are your most vivid experiences of church?
2. How do you feel on entering a church? Does it matter what the church is, or what it is like?
3. How can we make our church a more welcoming place?
4. Have you a personal Pentecost?

LARGE GROUP

Deal with any questions or comments from the Small Groups. After practical matters have been discussed, arrange a time for prayer.

PRAYER

Say together quietly:

'Come, Holy spirit, fill the hearts of the faithful.
Kindle in them the fire of your love.
Send forth your Spirit,
and they shall be created.
And you shall renew the face of the earth.'

The Leader should then invite everyone to open their hearts, in silence, to receive the Holy Spirit. He/she says: 'Let all minds be set on God's power, and our receptiveness. Repeat the words "Come, Holy Spirit" to yourself, and let the silence be broken only if and when someone feels the need to share a "word of the Lord".'

After a suitable period, conclude with everyone saying together:

'Holy Spirit of God,
sent by the Father and the Son,
fill my heart with your love.
Lead me to know myself,
to root out my selfishness,
and to share with others the fruits of your presence;
love, joy, peace, patience, kindness,
goodness, trustfulness, gentleness and self-control.'

(Bishop David Konstant, cf. *Galatians 5:22*, from *Jesus Christ: the Way, the Truth, the Life*.)

Unit 9
The Church's Story

The Church in the New Testament

The Christian Church, born at Pentecost, began with **Jewish people** who accepted Jesus as the Messiah continuing with their traditional faith and worship – in synagogues and the Temple. But they also met in each other's homes to celebrate the breaking of bread (= the Eucharist) as at Jesus' Last Supper. Much Christian worship today (prayers, blessings, gestures) reflects these Jewish roots.

However, those Christians (first so-called in Antioch, see *Acts 11:26*) were thought to be **heretics** (= holding unacceptable beliefs) by those who were not. By A.D. 85 Christians were no longer welcomed in synagogues. By this time though, the Christian community had had to cope with the problem of Gentile converts. Was it necessary to become Jewish before becoming Christian, or was baptism alone sufficient? This thorny problem was resolved at the first **Council**, when the Church leaders gathered in Jerusalem in A.D. 45 (read this in *Acts 15:1-35*). Jerusalem's first **Bishop**, James, passed a ruling which enabled the Church to spread throughout the Gentile world without obliging converts first to become Jews.

Growth and risks

The Church quickly spread within the Roman Empire, particularly through the tireless missionary efforts of St Paul. Through his letters and other New Testament books, we can glimpse life as it was for those early Christians. We see that they celebrated the Eucharist with words we still use today (*1 Corinthians 11:17-34*). They were 'united, heart and soul; no one claimed private ownership of any possessions, as everything they owned was held in common'. (*Acts 4:32, New Jerusalem Bible version*) They collected money for other churches in need (*II Corinthians 8 and 9*). They baptised all those who were prepared to risk everything, even their lives, to join them as members of the Church. Indeed, hundreds were to die as **martyrs** (= witnesses) for refusing to worship the Roman Emperor as a god.

Getting organised

To survive and be effective in spreading the Good News, the need for organisation was soon felt. Each baptised member had to take responsibility in some way, for the good of the whole group. To lead the group was a **bishop**, who had been taught or ordained by an apostle. When the group grew and formed new branches as time went on, **priests** would be put in charge of them, to deputise for the bishop.

The roles of bishops and priests gradually developed to adapt to changing circumstances. A particular change was to occur when many monks became ordained as priests in the great monasteries which spread throughout Europe in the Middle Ages. But, to return to the earliest days of the Church, **Deacons** would help the bishop during the **liturgy** (= service, worship by the people), and women too, with the baptisms, and in distributing the gifts provided for the needy (see *1 Timothy 3:8-13*). Many other **orders** and **ministries** were developed: elders, widows, gate-keepers, catechists (= those who teach by sharing their faith), sponsors, readers – and whatever else was necessary. Some of these survive today, while others are being rediscovered or adapted. (See Unit 16 for more details.)

Storms and freedom

The Christian Church rode the storms of bitter persecutions, and by the year A.D. 300 was found in all parts of the Roman world. Shortly after this date, following the last and worst persecution of all, under Emperor Diocletian, two events occurred which were to rock the world. In A.D. 313, two years after the Edict of Toleration, banning persecution of Christians, came the momentous Edict of Milan, in which the Emperors of both East and West granted religious freedom to the Church. The Western Emperor, Constantine the Great, not only became Christian himself, but prepared the way for a later Emperor (Theodosius) to make Christianity the **official religion of the Empire**. By the end of the sixth century Christianity was firmly established as far west as Ireland, and had spread to Southern India, Ethiopia and even Central China. Whole peoples and armies were turning to Christianity by **choice** or **force**. And there lay trouble.

Heresies and councils

Whilst small communities of highly committed people could ensure strict control over important matters of faith and behaviour, large numbers of reluctant or superficial Christians could easily be led astray. At times there was real confusion about what the Church believed. Many people were drawn to teachings which were not the same as those preached by the apostles. Great numbers, for example, followed the heresy of **Arius**, who maintained that Jesus was not truly God, but inferior to God. **Nestorius,** Bishop of Constantinople, taught incorrectly that there were two persons in Christ, a divine and a human, so that Mary could be called Mother of Christ, but not Mother of God!

Yet others were misled by **Docetism**, the idea that Jesus was really God, but only *seemed* to be human, and so could not suffer pain or have other human feelings. As the dangerous confusions arose, the Church leaders met together as they had done in Jerusalem in A.D. 45, and dealt with them by a series of **Councils** under the leadership of the Bishop of Rome, successor to the leading apostle, Peter. The conclusions of the Councils are accepted as having the authority of the Holy Spirit's guidance, and so are **infallible** (= incapable of being wrong). Some of these conclusions were in the form of **Creeds**, statements to be recited by Christians to express their true beliefs. The one produced by the Council of Nicaea in A.D. 325 which dealt with the heresy of Arius is the one said or sung at every Sunday Mass to this day.

Nestorius' views were countered by the Council of Ephesus in A.D. 431 which taught that Christ is a single person with two natures: human and divine. Mary is the Mother of Jesus, the person; therefore she is the Mother of God. The following Council, held in Chalcedon in A.D. 451, took on the Docetists by insisting that Christ was truly human as well as being God. Not only would the Church encourage devotion to the holiness of Christ, present in the Eucharist, but also would stress the real human sufferings felt by Jesus at his crucifixion, through certain forms of prayer (e.g. Stations of the Cross, the rosary and so on) and art. Realistic figures depicting the tortured Jesus on the cross were, and are, widespread reminders that the Son really, physically, suffered for love of us.

Saints and sinners

Councils are not the only means for keeping the Christian religion true to the Spirit of its Founder. There have been times (rather a lot!) when scandals and divisions, corruption and cruelty, ignorance and indifference scarred the face of the Church. Yet in the darkest times, the motherly Spirit has brought forth countless saints and scholars, reformers and simple people whose influence for good would bring the Christian people back to true worship and belief (see also **Saints** on page 66).

Some leading members of the Church

Bishops

The Bishop, who is the leading 'Shepherd-Priest' of the local area, has as his main job to preach and teach the Gospel, and to care for the priests and people within his **Diocese** (= area). He does all that a priest can do, and he also ordains priests and confirms candidates. He often consults groups of priests and lay people, visits parishes, commissions people to a variety of ministries, and sees his brother-bishop, the Pope, every five years. He discusses issues with the other bishops of his country at twice-yearly national **Conferences**. He may be sent as a representative to **International Synods**. If a **Council** is called, he will take part. Together the world's bishops form a **College** of equal partners in communion with the Pope, and are to the Church today what the apostles were in their time.

Deans

These priests have certain responsibilities in looking after groups of parishes in an area *within* the Diocese. A Diocese can be broken down into many Deaneries, or administrative units. (Do you know which Deanery *you* are in?)

The Pope

The word 'pope' (from the Latin for 'papa', as small children would call their father) was used till the sixth century of all bishops, before becoming reserved for the Bishop of Rome, as head of the Church on earth.

In this Church of Christ the Roman Pontiff* is the successor of Peter, to whom Christ entrusted the feeding of His sheep and lambs. Hence by divine institution he enjoys supreme, full, immediate, and universal authority over the care of souls. Since he is pastor of all the faithful, his mission is to provide for the common good of the universal Church and for the good of the individual churches.
(Decree on the *Bishops' Pastoral Office in the Church*, n. 2, Vatican II)

---

* *Pontiff = 'bridge-builder'.*

A Council for Our Times
The Second Vatican Council (1962-1965)

In 1959 a new Pope, John XXIII, announced that he would call together the twenty-first Ecumenical Council of the Church. Bishops from every part of the world and their theological advisers, observers from other Churches, and a few lay people, attended the four sessions of the Council from 1962 to 1965 which aimed at making decisions to help to renew the Church. Pope John was succeeded after the first session by Pope Paul VI who continued the Council in the same spirit as Pope John. By the end of the Council, sixteen documents had been produced, the most important being the four Constitutions: on the *Sacred Liturgy*, on *Divine Revelation*, on *The Church*, and on *The Church in the Modern World*.

'In its pilgrimage on earth, Christ summons the Church to continual reformation, of which it is always in need, in so far as it is an institution of human beings here on earth.'
(*Decree on Ecumenism*, n. 6)

Group Session

LARGE GROUP

In twos, spend ten minutes 'brainstorming' on *either*:

a) everything you know about the twelve apostles/ disciples, and what specific instructions Jesus gave them;

or

b) everything you know about any of the saints, and particularly why they are so.

SMALL GROUPS

Share the findings of the above. Further questions could bring out:

- How are the Lord's instructions carried out now?
- How are major questions settled now?
- How does authority work now?
- How is the Lord made present now?

LARGE GROUP

People holding various positions in the Church organisation could be invited to describe their role *briefly*, taking questions. The many ministries in the early Church could be described and then briefly 'experienced' by *all* present being allotted roles, on a 'hands-up' basis – as if the group constituted one of those early communities. (For further details of this exercise, see *The way we were*, Joppa, by Rev Michael Fewell.)

This exercise could be extended to take up most of a session, but some preparation is needed. After the exercise, take any questions or comments, and deal with practical matters. Finally, arrange a time for prayer.

PRAYER

When all are settled, have five good readers each take a section from *Isaiah 55*. (It is important that there are substantial *pauses* between each reading.)

Voice 1: verses 1-2
Voice 2: verses 3-5
Voice 3: verses 6-9
Voice 4: verses 10-11
Voice 5: verses 12-13

Allow for a period of **silence**, for all to make the reading their own. Conclude with everyone saying together the following prayer:

Lord Jesus Christ, Son of the living God,
teach us to walk in your Way more trustfully,
to accept your Truth more faithfully,
and to share your Life more lovingly.
By the power of the Holy Spirit
help us in our work for the Church
so that we may come as one family
to the kingdom of the Father,
where you live for ever and ever. Amen.

UNIT 10
Catholic
Specialities

Why Catholics make a special feature of:

Pictures and crucifixes

Because of its belief in Jesus as the Son of God made man, the Church believes that the whole of creation has been touched or 'graced' by his presence, and is therefore holy. Certain things are used by Catholics in their private, devotional prayer life as **aids**. These are different from the sacraments in that they are purely personal. They do not reflect the Faith as do the sacraments. They are called **sacramentals**, and include a wide variety of **devotional objects**, such as pictures, statues, crucifixes, holy water, palms, etc.

Gestures and **signs** also aid devotion by reminding us, at an unconscious level, of central elements of belief. For instance, touching holy water and making the sign of the cross on entering church links the ideas of the cleansing and new life of baptism with the name of the Holy Trinity, symbolically fitting us to enter a holy space.

The custom of tracing the cross with the thumb over forehead, lips and heart before hearing the Gospel during Mass reminds us to attune our thoughts, words and feelings to the crucified Word we shall encounter in the reading.

Anything which helps people to pray becomes part of the rich treasury of the Church's life on which following generations may draw.

Candles

Candles play a large part in Catholic culture. They burn with a living flame, and so indicate **life**. As a symbol of the new and risen life of Jesus, the special Easter or Paschal candle is used. At Mass, candles on the altar are lit to symbolise Jesus as the light of the world, and to link our present-day Eucharists with those of the early Church in the catacombs. Candles help to create a sense of occasion, and used to be carried in procession before the Roman Emperors as a mark of respect, as today they are carried before the Book of the Gospels. Candles may also be used to symbolise a particular prayer, in which case they are called 'votive' candles, and are usually lit in front of the statue of a saint whose help is being sought.

Purgatory

Exactly what life is like after death is not really knowable, until we die. So we are obliged to use the language and imagery of what we do know well in order to help us make sense of this mystery. We know that to come into the direct presence of God (= be in heaven) we need to be released from whatever selfishness and sin still clings to and disfigures us at death – for (of heaven) 'nothing unclean may come into it' (*Revelation 21:27*). This process of release, or 'purging', is seen by Christians of the Eastern tradition as one of growth towards maturity, whilst in the West, the language is more like that of a legal 'sentence'. We pray during Mass for those who have died: 'Bring them and all the departed into the light of your presence' (*Eucharistic Prayer II*).

Saints

In the New Testament 'saints' meant simply members of a particular Church. Today, the term is applied rather to those who are already in heaven. They, and particularly the Mother of Jesus, Mary, have played a large part in Catholic belief and culture. Their importance stems from the Catholic way of seeing the Church as a family which stretches back in time and includes those who have lived and died before us, and who are now enjoying the direct presence of God. If we value someone in life and pray for their well-being, it seems natural to continue to do so after their death, also to enlist their own prayer for us.

The 'Hail Mary'

Enlisting the prayer of the Church's Number One Saint, Mary, is involved in this popular and ancient prayer which is largely based on Scripture. The greetings to Mary by the Archangel Gabriel and by Elizabeth in *Luke 1:28 and 42* form the first half, which was in use by Christians of the fifth century. 'Hail Mary, full of grace. The Lord is with thee. Blessed art thou among women and blessed is the fruit of thy womb, Jesus.' The second half, added and in use by the sixteenth century, petitions Mary to pray on our behalf. The term **Mother of God** reminds us of both the humanity and the divinity of Jesus. By saying 'us sinners' we are acknowledging our own share in the world's suffering and our solidarity with each other. 'Holy Mary, mother of God, pray for us sinners, now and at the hour of our death. Amen.'

The Rosary

To pray the rosary is to be engaged in prayer at many levels. Spoken prayers are 'counted off' by means of beads strung in a particular pattern. Meanwhile, the imagination is involved in meditating on each of the fifteen **Mysteries**, or events in the life, death and resurrection of Christ Jesus, seen, as it were, through his mother's eyes. The fifteen subjects are grouped into three sections:

- the Joyful, concerning the birth and early life of Jesus;
- the Sorrowful, focusing on his suffering and death;
- the Glorious, involved with the Resurrection and its consequences.

Each of these sections is made up of five specific events. Each event is contemplated during the recitation of the *Lord's Prayer* and ten *Hail Marys*, one bead counted off with every prayer. The sequence of ten *Hail Marys*, called a **decade**, is concluded with a 'Glory be . . . (to the Father, and to the Son and to the Holy Spirit, as it was in the beginning, is now and ever shall be, world without end. Amen.)'

By the time you have 'prayed your way' round the rosary once, you will have said five decades, and pondered five mysteries. To pray the complete rosary you would go round it three times, saying altogether fifteen *Our Fathers*, fifteen *God bes*, and no fewer than one hundred and fifty *Hail Marys* – in fact, the number of psalms there are in the Bible. This 'devotion', or form of prayer, was developed by people in the Middle Ages who wished to join the monks in reciting the 150 psalms which they prayed regularly, but, as the ordinary people could not read Latin, they joined with the monks by repeating the *Hail Mary* instead.

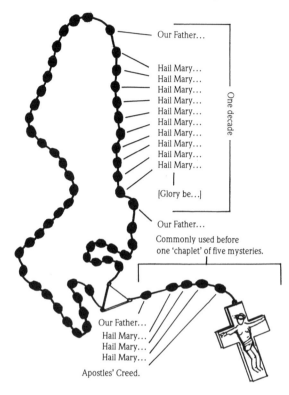

Our Father...

Hail Mary...
Hail Mary...
Hail Mary...
Hail Mary...
Hail Mary...
Hail Mary...
Hail Mary...
Hail Mary...
Hail Mary...
Hail Mary...

One decade

[Glory be...]

Our Father...

Commonly used before one 'chaplet' of five mysteries.

Our Father...
Hail Mary...
Hail Mary...
Hail Mary...

Apostles' Creed.

Group Session

LARGE GROUP

Welcome everyone. If this has not been done already, why not conduct a **guided tour** of the Catholic church, pointing out specific items and explaining their role? Try to include the sacristy and confessionals. A display of vestments and altar furniture may be of interest. Even lifelong Catholics may value such an exploration!

Review the theme, picking up comments and questions from the Group.

SMALL GROUPS

Suggested topics for discussion:

- What helps you to remember your loved ones?
- In prayer, is it easier for you to address someone you can *see* represented by a picture or statue?
- How necessary or desirable do you think it is for 'holy art' to be of a high standard?

- How comfortable do you feel with certain Catholic 'specialities'? Do any of them bother or puzzle you?
- Do you feel that too much or too little attention is paid to these 'specialities'?
- Which other practices would you like to have explained . . . (prepare for the Large Group)?

LARGE GROUP

Take up any questions or comments arising from the Small Groups' discussions. There may be requests to have explained such things as: limbo; incense; bells; genuflections; 'First Fridays'; Novenas; miraculous medals; referring to a priest as 'Father'; etc.

There may be confusion over why the Church bans horoscopes, astrologers and so forth; and why, 'as the Vatican has so much wealth, there seem to be "poor" parishes'.

After practical matters have been dealt with, move into prayer.

PRAYER

All say together the *Our Father* (traditional version); then, in silence, each person should say it to him/herself *slowly*. Then, all say it together word by word, or phrase by phrase, *very* slowly, pausing between each. Eventually, when each word has had time to 'soak in', just be still, and allow time for members to ponder on any words or phrases which come into their minds.

After a suitable period (as long as can be sustained) conclude with invoking the help of Our Lady, by everyone saying together the *Hail Mary*.

Hail Mary, full of grace.
The Lord is with thee.
Blessed art thou among women,
and blessed is the fruit of thy womb, Jesus.
Holy Mary, Mother of God, pray for us, sinners,
now, and at the hour of our death. Amen.

UNIT 11
Prayer

In the Bible we find the story of God seeking to bring about human fulfilment throughout history. Sometimes God is pictured as a jealous lover looking for his unfaithful spouse; sometimes as a keen gardener, a vinekeeper who lavishes his time on his favourite plant, only to find that it produces little fruit; at other times God is seen as a shepherd who cares for his sheep with love. Throughout the Scriptures God is seen as caring for all that he has created with such love, and invites from humanity a similar caring and a loving response, a **relationship**.

In our lives the unfolding story of this relationship is called **prayer**. It is our response to the God who is already looking for us, and waiting eagerly for us to turn to him. In prayer we do not force God to listen to us; instead we try to make ourselves available to God, to listen, to allow God to speak to us. Prayer is always God's work more than it is our own. He draws us to himself. We do not have to set out to capture him.

God is always closer to us than we can imagine. His intentions for us are always good; in prayer we try to open up ourselves to him as he really is, not as we would like him to be. Anything that expresses our relationship with God, any thought or action, is prayer. It is always an act of faith or trust that God really exists, and that he really is as he has shown himself to be. God is not out to deceive or trick us; he loves us, and so we surrender ourselves to him in love. The surrender is prayer.

The way **Jesus** prayed brings a new dimension to prayer. He is seen in the Gospels as addressing God with ease, with intimacy, and with a name. The Jews refused, out of respect, to use God's name, but Jesus calls him **Father** with a word that appears in our language as 'Daddy' – Abba. Jesus chats to the Father like a child, always with confidence, secure in the knowledge of the Father's love. At times he asks the Father to change his plans, as in his prayer in Gethsemane, but always he puts what the Father wants before his own fears.

Jesus' own way of praying was taken up by the Church and kept for us in what we call the *Lord's Prayer*

('Our Father'). It is full of confidence that God is a loving Father, and that he does listen to his children.

The Church teaches that Jesus' whole life was a prayer to the Father. The supreme moment of prayer was that of Jesus on the Cross when his prayer then was the voice of prayer of all humanity. As the one Mediator between God and people, Christ's prayer is always heard. When we join our prayers to his, we can be sure that our prayer finds acceptance. For this reason all the official prayers of the Church finish with the words 'through Christ'. St Paul describes the Spirit as bringing about our closeness to Jesus. He says that the Spirit leads us to imitate the prayer of Jesus, and so we too can come to trust God as a loving Father, and see him as anxious to give his children all they need.

When we pray consciously, that is by giving time to it apart from our living and acting, we can pray with **praise** and **thanksgiving**. That means to speak to God as the creator, to see ourselves as part of his plan. We can pray with **contrition**; that is to admit our failures to live as part of his plan. We can pray with **petition**, meaning that we become more sensitive to the needs of others, and more sensitive to the ways in which we can help them.

Catholic Christians see prayer as having a special awareness that we are a **people**, that God has called a people to himself, and so we pray as part of a large family. This is expressed best of all at Mass: the **Eucharist** (thanksgiving) is the great expression of thanks from the Church to the Father 'through Christ'.

'This "liturgy" (or public activity) is the summit towards which the activity of the Church is directed; it is also the fount from which all her power flows.' (Vatican Council document on *Sacred Liturgy*, n. 10). By celebrating the Eucharist and the 'Divine Office', 'the Church is ceaselessly engaged in praising the Lord and interceding for the salvation of the entire world.' (*Sacred Liturgy*, n. 83)

The **Divine Office** is the official, public, prayer of the Church. The elements in it are Morning Prayer and

Evening Prayer, although Compline, or Night Prayers is also very popular. Each Prayer follows a fixed programme of psalms, Scripture readings, hymns and intercessions. Over a four-week period, all the psalms in the Bible will have been said, sung, chanted or read silently by priests, religious Sisters and Brothers, and lay people, either in groups or by themselves. At any time, someone, somewhere in the world will be offering to God the due praise of his people!

Group Session

LARGE GROUP

Welcome everyone; review the theme. Team members, or others, could offer very brief explanations of different forms of prayer as experienced and practised by many Catholics today.

Examples might include:

- Charismatic Prayer
- Meditation on Scripture, Lord's Prayer, Titles of God, etc.
- Healing Prayer (e.g. of memories)
- Bidding Prayers (Prayer of the Faithful)
- The Rosary
- Litanies
- Prayers for (some of) the Stations of the Cross
- The Jesus Prayer

Other examples may well arise during future sessions. Remember that there is a rich seam to be mined that cannot possibly be attempted in one, or even fifty sessions!

SMALL GROUPS

Discussion may be helped by using the following questions:

1. Is there a way of prayer, that you have found to be helpful, which you could share?
2. What difficulties do you find with prayer?
3. Is it more important to you to 'say prayers' or to pray?

4. When may knowing a number of 'set' prayers be helpful? Which do you cherish, or dislike?
5. Have there been circumstances in your life which have been affected by prayer?
6. Can you pray 'among the pots and pans' (as St Teresa of Avila expressed it), or do you need a special time and place?

LARGE GROUP

Take any comments or questions from the Group. Deal with any practical matters. Then, before creating the **prayer space**, invite suggestions for the method of prayer to be used this session. If opinions vary, then each person will have to pray quietly in her/his own way for the next few moments, when the Prayer begins.

PRAYER

After a time, conclude with everyone saying together the Magnificat:

My soul glorifies the Lord,
my spirit rejoices in God, my Saviour.
He looks on his servant in her lowliness:
henceforth all ages will call me blessed.
The Almighty works marvels for me. Holy his name!
His mercy is from age to age, on those who fear him.
He puts forth his arm in strength,
and scatters the proud-hearted.
He casts the mighty from their thrones,
and raises the lowly.
He fills the starving with good things,
and sends the rich away empty.
He protects Israel, his servant,
remembering his mercy,
the mercy promised to our fathers,
to Abraham and his sons forever.

UNIT 12
Sign and Sacrament

Even with our contemporary scientific and materialistic minds we still consider some things to be good ways of expressing ourselves. Flowers can mean, 'I'm sorry', 'Happy Birthday/Anniversary' or 'Thank you'.

Poetry performs the same task. 'My love is like a red, red rose.' Robert Burns was not implying that his beloved was bright crimson, rather that, just as he feels when he sees a lovely rose in June, so he feels when he sees his girl. The most intimate and personal things are often best expressed in this way, i.e. by **symbolic words**, or by a **sign** or **gesture**. We greet people by shaking their hands; we express affection with a kiss, anger with a clenched fist. All these are part of our symbolic language.

The **Church** has a similar symbolic language in speaking about God; it is a language of signs and symbols. We call it a **sacramental language**. We believe that God cannot be seen by men, but that he has given us a sign of himself – Jesus, whom St Paul calls the 'image of the unseen God', and so we say that Jesus is the Sacrament of God, that is the sign or **token** by which God makes himself present to us.

Christian art also helps us, by expressing in images the same truth that the Gospels communicate in words. 'We declare that we preserve intact all the written and unwritten traditions of the Church which have been entrusted to us. One of these traditions consists in the production of representational artwork, which accords with the history of the preaching of the Gospel. For it confirms that the incarnation of the Word of God was real and not imaginary.' (*Council of Nicaea II*)

Listening to the words of Scripture and of prayer, singing hymns, contemplating sacred art, and being involved in symbolic gestures and actions – all help to take our minds and hearts beyond our immediate concerns, so that we can enter more deeply into the celebrations of they mystery of Christ.

We need to be careful not to use the words 'sign', 'symbol' and 'token' as meaning something that is not quite true: 'It's only a symbol, or a token gesture.' These phrases often mean that something is slightly false, or less than real. When the Church uses its sacramental language it means that it is trying to express something very real and powerful by means of a sign. Symbol is the deepest form of reality. Scripture shows Jesus himself as using very ordinary food and drink, and the simple action of laying on of hands, to serve as 'symbols' of the extra-ordinary, loving power of God.

Just as we believe **Jesus** to be the **Sacrament of God** (i.e. the best way of making God present to us), so Catholics say that the **Church** is the **Sacrament of Christ**. That means that we will find the clearest expression of his life and work in the Church, which is his Body, through which he acts and speaks and heals and reconciles and gives life.

The Sacraments

The word **sacrament** for Catholics has now come to describe certain activities of the Church which express the presence of Christ acting in her. There are seven of these activities in the Catholic Church:

- Baptism
- Confirmation
- Eucharist
- Penance (Reconciliation)
- Orders
- Marriage
- Anointing of the Sick

- The sacraments, therefore, are the signs which express our faith in the reality hidden underneath them;
- they are the signs through which we worship and encounter God intimately;
- they are the signs of the unity of the Church, because they express what the whole Church believes, not just our private devotions;
- they are the signs of Christ being present in his Body, the Church;
- they provide opportunities for celebrating the presence of God in the significant times of our life and in the life of the Church.

The seven sacraments which we have now were defined as such by St Thomas Aquinas, and subsequently by the Council of Trent in the sixteenth century. The form of each sacrament has altered many times down the ages, the most recent renewal being undertaken after the Vatican Council in the 1960s.

Each sacrament consists of an **activity accompanied by prayer**, e.g. baptism is a washing with water in the name of the Trinity; anointing is a rubbing with oil accompanied by a prayer of healing. This is the essential part of a sacrament: the activity with the words. The ceremonial way in which this activity is presented will vary from age to age and culture to culture. The sacraments are always **public celebrations** belonging to the whole Community of the Church. They are not private devotions.

Even sacraments which do not *seem* to affect anybody else (for example, penance, or healing) really do so. As everyone who has been baptised (or entered into the process leading to baptism), has been made a part of the one Body, one Family, of Christ, then the whole Body is affected by the state of health of every single member of it – just as a piece of grit in the eye, or a toothache, can bring low a sturdy six-footer!

A sacrament is a festive action in which Christians assemble to celebrate their lived experience and to call to heart their common story. The action is a symbol of God's care for us in Christ. Enacting the symbol brings us closer to one another in the Church and to the Lord who is there for us.
(Tad Guzie, *The Book of Sacramental Basics*)

Group Session

LARGE GROUP

Welcome everyone; review the theme. In a 'brainstorming' session, encourage members to give their ideas on:

• What are some of the symbols used in everyday life?

- What are they saying, in ways other than in words?
- What celebrations publicly affirm a matter of significance in the life of a nation, community, family or personal life? Are they ritualised in any way? What effects are they intended to have on the participants?
- Is it possible to celebrate a tragedy?

SMALL GROUPS

Suggestions for dicussion topics:

1. Are you able to celebrate special occasions within the family? Does your family ever share a meal together?
2. Have you ever experienced a real sense of celebration at a civic or religious service?
3. Does the use of symbols help you to celebrate? If so how?
4. Sacraments provide us with occasions for celebrating God's presence. In what other ways can we celebrate God's presence in our lives?

LARGE GROUP

Take any questions and comments from the groups. Invite suggestions for symbols which people would like to explore, e.g. water, oil, wedding rings, sign of the cross, etc. (They may be dealt with more fully in future sessions, but now could be an appropriate time for introducing the riches of symbolic meanings.)

PRAYER

Leader:
either

Use a common symbol (a lighted candle, an open Bible, a cross, a plant) as the focus for reflection. Set it in the centre, where all can see. Remove other distractions. Invite people to concentrate their attention and imagination on that focus, thanking God while allowing the symbol to work silently upon them. Some quiet background music may be helpful.

or

Give all present the opportunity to choose a symbol (picture, cross, etc.) from a selection before them, and then to concentrate on their prayer, using the symbol to focus their attention.

Encourage them to talk quite naturally to God the Father as they pray. After a while, invite any who wish to do so to share an insight or reflection. Conclude with everyone saying together the *Prayer of St Ignatius*:

> Teach us, good Lord,
> to serve you as you deserve;
> to give and not to count the cost,
> to fight and not to heed the wounds,
> to toil and not to seek for rest,
> to labour and not to ask for any reward,
> save that of knowing that we do your will;
> through Jesus Christ our Lord. Amen.

UNIT 13
Baptism and
Confirmation

Baptism

The word **baptism** comes from a Greek word which means 'to bathe, dip or plunge in water'. The English evangelist, Trevor Dearing, in a light-hearted moment, once likened baptism to the action of becoming a 'Holy tea-bag'! – plunged into the water to enable 'all the flavour to come flooding through!'

Seriously, baptism is laden with a wealth of symbolic meaning and significance. Water, which sustains life, can also kill. Being submerged in it, even for a religious purpose, can convey the impression of undergoing a form of 'death'. 'Dying' and 'rising' as well as being ritually cleansed and purified; these images have all been used by the Church, as they have by many religious traditions, to mark the stage of admission, or initiation through total repentance and conversion. In the Gospels we see Jesus being baptised by John the Baptist.

Many years later the Gospel writers linked this event with what happened to the apostles at Pentecost, when the Holy Spirit was 'poured out' on them. The early Church thus introduced baptism in the name of Jesus as the way of receiving his Spirit, and thereby joining the community which met in his name for teaching and the breaking of bread. So initiation into the Church was made up of the following: water baptism – outpouring of the Spirit – Eucharist. This is still the pattern today. The three Sacraments of Baptism, Confirmation and Eucharist make up the Sacraments of Initiation into the Church.

By the sacrament of Baptism . . . [a person] becomes truly incorporated into the crucified and glorified Christ, and is reborn to a sharing of the divine life.
(*Decree on Ecumenism*, n. 22, Vatican II)

According to the Acts of the Apostles large numbers of people were baptised with no preparation beyond a 'profession of faith', the declaration of their belief in Jesus as the Christ. As the Church began to meet hostility and persecution there emerged a structure for preparing people for initiation into the Church. In order to test the seriousness of a person's interest in the Church, and also to weed out the possible entry of spies into the community, as well as eliminating as far as possible the scandal of apostasy (the public denial of Christ by a Christian), the Church began a **catechumenate**. This provided a lengthy period of preparation for prospective members, and celebrated their gradual acceptance into the community by means of certain rituals, until the solemn moment during the Easter celebration when they received the Sacraments of Baptism, Confirmation and Eucharist together, and so became fully initiated members. There was also a long period of after-care for the continuing involvement of the newcomer into the life of the community.

If we are silent about the joy which comes from knowing about Jesus, the very stones of our cities will cry out! For we are an Easter people and 'Alleluia' is our song.
(John Paul II, after the words of St Augustine)

After the year A.D. 313 persecution of Christians ceased, and Christianity gradually became the official religion of the empire. Within a hundred years, the catechumenate was becoming redundant, as newly born babies began to make up the majority of new entrants to the Church. This became the norm, especially with the growing feeling that baptism was necessary for freeing the infant from the guilt of the sin of Adam and Eve: **'original sin'**. So the practice emerged of baptism for new-born babies, followed some years later by confirmation and finally Eucharist. This was the situation until early this century when the Pope wished to make Holy Communion available to children, and so the order in which the sacraments are received was reversed; now the order for Catholics most commonly is baptism, Eucharist, confirmation. The Orthodox Churches give all three initiation sacraments to babies.

During the first four centuries, therefore, the understanding of the sacrament underwent a deep change: from being a public entry into a community of faith to being a personal need for the cancellation of original sin.

Since the Second Vatican Council there has been an attempt to reverse this process. Once more the necessity of faith is being emphasised. Baptism is the celebration of a living faith; so even in the case of babies there must be some faith to celebrate. Hence the emphasis on the faith of the parents and sponsors.

As well as original sin there is also **'original grace'**, which is a more ancient idea. This means that human nature, and everything about our life and this world, has been 'graced' by the presence of Christ in it. He was the fully mature man, the perfect human being. He invites us to become more fully human, to accept the human condition, to journey through life with its risks and possible failures by living a way of life which he has shown us: a life that does not end with death. He invites us, in fact, to live our lives by the same power with which he lived his – the Holy Spirit. We receive this power to begin the lifelong journey with him through our baptism.

Also, since the Council, there has been the re-introduction of the **catechumenate** as the normal means of receiving adult converts into the Church. This means that their progress is once again the responsibility of the whole community and not just of one priest. Their gradual initiation is accompanied by liturgical celebrations until their full initiation takes place at the Easter Vigil.

Confirmation

Originally the celebration of the Sacraments of Initiation was led by the bishop in the cathedral at Easter. With the enormous increase in the number of Christians during the fourth century, the bishops delegated the baptism and Eucharist parts of the rite to the priests. Each bishop undertook to supply the part where he lays hands upon the baptised, prays for the descent of the Holy Spirit upon them (again) with the special oil or 'chrism'. He was to do this as soon after baptism as possible, but in the conditions of the times, it frequently took place only after a period of years: this part became known as **confirmation**. Bishops can now delegate priests to confirm adults during the Easter Vigil.

The words used at confirmation include 'be sealed with the gift of the Holy Spirit', and so it was seen as a means of perfecting or ratifying the baptism of those who were baptised years before, increasingly, as babies. By receiving the indwelling of the Holy Spirit, the **missionary** dimension of baptism and of the Church is given new focus.

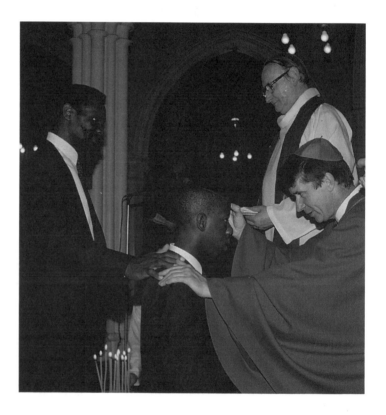

Confirmation now is a moment when the Church shows itself to the rest of the world as a particular kind of community (a community filled with the Spirit of God) which is dedicated to the transformation of the whole of creation by the release of the Spirit.

Group Session

LARGE GROUP

Welcome everyone; review the theme.

Either

Explore some of the **images** which illustrate the stages of the catechumenate:

exodus journey = oppression and escape; passing through the Red Sea – desert wandering, time of testing, covenanting, crossing Jordan; Promised Land where *begins* the history of Israel.

athlete = general training and fitness; trials – intensive training and preparation for the contest; title to maintain against all-comers.

marriage = dating and courtship; engagement – deepening the relationship in preparation for the wedding; enduring love, commitment renewed in daily interaction.

Any others?

Or

Explore the symbols of Easter/Baptism = Death/New Life, with special emphasis on **water**, e.g. stories of Noah and Jonah, and early Church practice. (The early Church required those being baptised to be submerged three times, after each confession of belief in the Father, Son and Holy Spirit. It must have felt to the wet and spluttering new Christian that he/she was close to being drowned! How might that experience teach them about dying to the 'old self' to be born anew in Christ?)

SMALL GROUPS

Suggestions for discussion topics:

1. In which situation do you feel a greatest sense of *belonging*? – family, village, club?
2. What *gives* you that sense of belonging?
3. Is what you belong to *open* to others, or closed? Does it matter?

4. What might encourage a real sense of belonging in the Church? Does it happen?
5. There is little actual *persecution* in the West against Christians, but in what ways may you meet discouragement? How do you cope?
6. How was your interest in faith/Church membership first kindled? When and how did you make a real choice?

LARGE GROUP

Take any questions and comments from the Small Groups. (If appropriate, discuss arrangements for the forthcoming liturgical rites for the catechumenate.)

PRAYER

After practical matters, arrange the prayer space and invite all to read quietly *Acts 2:1-4, 17-21*. It may help to have it read aloud by a good reader, stirringly! Remind everyone that such passages were written *for* them. Can this one be said to be *about* them? Ask them to consider this, reflectively, all the time praying to the Holy Spirit to make his home with them.

After an appropriate period, conclude by saying together the *Divine Praises*:

Blessed be God.
Blessed be his holy name.
Blessed be Jesus Christ, true God and true man.
Blessed be the name of Jesus.
Blessed be his most sacred heart.
Blessed be his most precious blood.
Blessed be Jesus in the most holy sacrament of the altar.
Blessed be the Holy Spirit, the Paraclete.
Blessed be the great mother of God, Mary most holy.
Blessed be her holy and immaculate conception.
Blessed be her glorious assumption.
Blessed be the name of Mary, virgin and mother.
Blessed be Saint Joseph, her spouse most chaste.
Blessed be God in his angels and in his saints.

UNIT 14
Eucharist (Mass)

This, the third of the three sacraments by which a member is initiated into the Catholic Church, is 'the source and summit' of the Christian life. The Body of Christ is assembled to express its praise and thanksgiving in the best way available. All the other sacraments in some way contribute to, and exist for, this purpose. The Body of Christ (the people) receives the Body of Christ (the Eucharist), to become more Christ-like, more like itself. The Word which was with God (*John 1*) comes into the world again, both as the word ('This is the word of the Lord') and as food ('for my flesh is real food' *John 6:55*). By actively receiving the Word in word and food, the Christian accepts the challenge to be Christ-like, to love as he loved.

The first Mass

When Jewish people celebrate the **Passover**, calling to heart the ancient liberation-event of their ancestors, it becomes a 'happening' in the present. They bring the past so powerfully into the present, that *they* are the slaves being called out from Egypt. Present experiences of oppression are seen through a fresh perspective, and so faith and hope are rekindled.

In the same way, each Mass is making real, here and now, the events which took place during the Passover in Jerusalem in or about A.D. 33. The Passover supper which Jesus shared with his friends, with all its foreshadowing of death and resurrection, was invested by Jesus with new significance.

The breaking of the bread finds echoes in the breaking of Christ's body on the cross. Sharing the separate pieces of what had been whole, speaks of Christ's sharing of his life with his friends, to make whole again the one Body. As grapes are crushed to produce wine, and as wine is poured out to be consumed, so the Cup of Acceptance, recalling the Covenant, is given new meaning as 'God's new covenant, sealed with my blood, which is poured out for you'. (*Luke 22:20*) Jesus, the Messiah, identified himself with the lamb which each household sacrificed. The blood of the lamb had been sprinkled on the doorposts originally so that the angel of death would **pass-over** and leave the household safe from death. In the Mass, liberation and life is offered again – not for one people alone, but for the whole world.

Mass today

Mass today can be celebrated
- by thousands in cathedrals, or basilicas,
- by a few friends in someone's home.

It may be in
- the open air
- a parish church or 'Mass Centre'
- schools, hospitals, prisons, factories . . .

The variety of ways in which Mass is celebrated is truly **catholic** – representing the tastes and traditions of all manner of people. The many different Eastern Catholic Rites worship in ways which, to western eyes and ears, seem very close to the Greek Orthodox. The musical tastes or customs of one community might drive another to distraction! Whereas early Sunday morning Mass-goers in Britain often prefer a 'quiet Mass', some South American Indian Mass-goers seem intent on being heard from the most distant mountains! Whereas Europeans **stand** for the Gospel as a mark of respect, Africans **sit** for the same reason!

Whatever the differences in styles as in people, what unites Catholics throughout the world is the real presence of Christ within their communities. For **communion** means not only being united with God but with each other equally too. The triumph of love, so dearly won by Jesus the Christ, is celebrated in the great Thanksgiving, which is the Eucharist.

Three important elements in any celebration of the Mass

1. Mass is not 'out there', but 'in here'. We are not called simply to look and listen, but to respond, to accept challenges, to risk being changed.

2. We are invited to share with Christ in a 'pass-over' from death to life, not for our sake only, but for the whole world.

3. The faith of those who celebrate is both expressed, and made real. The quality of our celebration will largely depend on the kind of Christian life we live. Celebrations are *underlined* moments of our lives. God is not fooled by 'instant switch-ons'!

The two great parts of the Mass

The two main parts of the Mass are called:

the **liturgy of the Word** – centred on encountering the Word of God in Scripture;
the **liturgy of the Eucharist** – encountering the Word of God in the sacrificial meal.

Introductory and **Concluding Rites** serve as a frame for the two parts. In the **Introductory Rites** we gather together, then sing an Entrance Song while the priest and ministers process to the altar. We are greeted by the priest, and then, to prepare ourselves for hearing the readings, we are called to **repent** (= change course) and trust in God's mercy.

In the **Liturgy of the Word** we then attend to the **readings** from Scripture:

(i) passage from the Old Testament
(ii) our response in the form of a psalm
(iii) passage from the New Testament
(iv) Gospel reading;

Hearing the word of God is only half the exercise. Listening to the word is the other half and that requires both effort and response from us.
(B. O'Connor, *Celebration in Faith*)

- we learn through the **homily** (= short talk) how to apply the readings to our daily lives. Good homilies have been known to change lives!
- we stand to **proclaim** our faith, knowing that some have been persecuted for doing just that;
- we **place our needs** and the needs of the world into the hands of God, knowing that the prayers of the saints join with ours.

The **Liturgy of the Eucharist** then begins with the preparation of gifts,
- we bring up gifts of bread and wine to the altar, forms under which Christ offers himself up to the Father for the sake of us all;
- we bring up gifts of money (the collection) which represent tokens of our work and activities, our daily lives;
- God is then blessed in the words of an ancient Jewish Blessing in thanks for the bread and wine.

Then begins the proclamation of the Eucharistic Prayer: 'The Eucharistic Prayer, a prayer of thanksgiving and sanctification, is the high point of the entire celebration. The meaning of the prayer is that the whole congregation joins Christ in acknowledging the works of God and offering the sacrifice.' (General Introduction to the *Roman Missal* 54)

In this prayer
- the Church calls to mind all God's good works in the past and expresses her hopes in God's faithfulness until the end of time
- the Church represents the words Jesus himself used during the Last Supper and in offering himself for the salvation of all
- the Church calls on the Holy Spirit to enable us to share God's life as we share the sacrificial meal

The past, present and future are all drawn into this great prayer as, at each Mass, the sacrifice of Christ on Calvary is renewed, though never repeated. The simple bread and wine have become the blessed sacrament, the body and blood of Christ. Then occurs **the breaking of the bread**. As the body of the crucified Jesus was broken for our sake, so, in the breaking of bread, we are given a sign to be broken for others. As we are all fed from the one loaf, so we are reminded of the need to be 'as one' with each other. Just before the bread is broken, we say together the Lord's Prayer and make our peace with those around us, normally by shaking hands.

We then accept the Lord's invitation to eat and to drink, to receive the **communion** sacrifice in order to participate fully in the mystery. We respond to the words 'The Body of Christ' and 'The Blood of Christ' with our 'Amen'. This is both our joyful acceptance of Christ's life and healing spirit, and our acceptance of the challenge to become more Christ-like, at whatever the cost. By its nature, sharing the Body of Christ in Holy Communion bonds us both with God and with the Church, the Body of Christ. It is the ultimate sign of unity.

In the **Concluding Rites**, after communion, we move naturally into areas of concern for the parish: notices are given about events, services, charities, meetings. It is right that prayer should lead to caring about others, not only in the parish, but beyond – wherever need is felt; with God's blessing and our thanks for having been together, we are sent out into the world like the apostles, to 'love and serve the Lord', which we can only do by loving and serving others.

Christ is present

At every Mass, Christ is present in different ways:

- in the Assembly of the People ('where two or three are gathered in my name, there I am in the midst of them');
- in the Word of God = the Scriptures (see also Unit 7);
- in the person of the priest, representing Christ for us;
- under the appearance of bread and wine:

> **The Eucharist is the silence of God, the weakness of God. To reduce himself to bread while the world is so noisy, so agitated, so confused . . . one needs really strong faith to understand the impotence and defeat which the Eucharist represents and which is today what the impotence and defeat of Calvary was yesterday. And yet this powerless Jesus, nailed down and annihilated, is the God of the impossible, Alpha and Omega, the beginning and the end.**
> (Carlo Carretto, *Letters from the Desert*)

Bread

We pray that the bread will 'become for us the bread of life'. The bread which we have made and offered will become the body of Christ broken for us on a cross, but because of that, leading us to share the resurrection. So we see that only by our being broken too for others are we obeying his instruction to 'go, and do likewise'. The life which the bread gives often takes us too by way of the cross.

One Body (the Church, made up of many people) is fed from one 'loaf' (Christ himself). As manna nourished the Israelites in the desert, so this Bread nourishes us today – yet making us also aware of the millions of God's people who have no bread, and who thus become our responsibility.

Wine

We pray that this wine will 'become for us our spiritual drink', the drink which brings the Holy Spirit into our lives. Wine, to Jesus and his friends, suggested two contrary images:

– It is associated with **pleasure**: 'You (God) bring forth food from the earth, and wine to cheer people's hearts' (*Psalm 104, NJB*); with feasting in the Promised Land, and at the banquet to be prepared when the Messiah comes, when 'a table will be prepared for me . . . and my cup (wineglass) will overflow' (*Psalm 23*). Jesus had changed water into wine at a wedding feast (see *John 2:1-10*) to show that he was bringing in the age of the Messiah himself; and feasting, eating and drinking are often used to indicate the joys of heaven, where Christ's kingdom is truly set.

– It is, however, also associated with **suffering, violent death, sacrifice**: Jesus asks his disciples, 'Can you drink of the cup from which I drink?' – meaning, are they prepared to risk the sufferings which he will have to undergo? Just before his arrest and execution, Jesus prays: 'May this cup pass from me'. So, when we receive the cup offered to us at Communion, by accepting and drinking, we are saying *yes* to his challenge: we will endure the consequences of being like Christ. Even if it means being put to death.

Communion Services

Sick and housebound Catholics are being brought Holy Communion to their homes or hospital beds by priests, deacons and by increasing numbers of lay people. These lay people have received training and been commissioned as Lay (or 'Extraordinary') Ministers of Communion.

Communion services, led by lay people, have also become part of the Church's life. Frequently now when a priest is not available in a parish, a Lay Minister will conduct a service at which people can receive Holy Communion. This will contain many of the parts of the Mass, except – of course – the Eucharistic Prayer. The lay minister has to use **hosts** (small wafers of bread) which have *already* been consecrated and stored in the locked cabinet of the **tabernacle**. (You can always tell that there are consecrated hosts in a tabernacle if there is a special lamp lit nearby.) Because there are fewer priests than there are Catholic communities, lay people perform a vital task in holding these services – even on Sundays. In many parts of the world, this is the normal practice, as a priest may be able to visit a community only on rare occasions. The Church ensures that the faithful are not deprived of receiving Our Lord in Communion.

Reservation of the Blessed Sacrament

Consecrated hosts are not only reserved in the tabernacle for use in Communion Services and for Communion to the sick. Such hosts are not just **bread** but are **Christ**

under the appearance of bread. They are reserved so that people can pray quietly in the 'Sacramental' presence of Christ himself. Sometimes one of the larger hosts is displayed in a **monstrance**, a glass-fronted portable display vessel, with gold or silver frame, usually of a 'sunburst' design. Catholics find that praying before a host is a powerful help to concentration and a constant reminder of God's self-giving love to us. Usually this display ends with **Benediction**, a short service originating in the Middle Ages, in honour of the Blessed Sacrament.

Some frequently asked questions

1. *Is Mass the time for private prayer?* There is a sense in which people should be praying throughout the whole of Mass, concentrating on the action of the Mass. The time to pray individual prayers, other than when invited to do so at the Bidding Prayers or for those we know who have died, is between Masses. Mass is a time for the whole community to pray together, rather than for each of us to pray privately.

2. *Should there be silence at Mass?* There are breaks in the Mass for people to collect their thoughts and consider what has been said or done, and this is easier if the church is quiet. However, we should be tolerant of noise-makers, as well as be sensitive to fellow worshippers.

3. *Can Communion be received more than once on the same day?* So long as you participate in the whole service, you can receive Communion more than once. You should not just 'dash in' for Communion!

4. *Why do some people receive Communion in their hands and others in their mouths?* It was the custom for a time for Communion always to be 'on the tongue', but now it is a matter of individual choice.

5. *Are people only receiving 'half' Communion if they receive in only one 'kind' (i.e. only the consecrated bread, or 'Host')?* No, Communion is complete if only one kind is received, but restoring the traditional practice of Communion in both kinds allows a more perfect re-creation of the Last Supper.

Group Session

LARGE GROUP

Welcome everyone; review the theme. If possible, show some of the excellent audiovisual aids on this subject, e.g. set of slides on the Mass by Bishop David Konstant.

Invite contributions on the 'highlights' of the Mass; write them up (on blackboard or large sheets of paper) to reveal the shape of the liturgy.

Explore the four Eucharistic Prayers, explain the differences between them, etc.

SMALL GROUPS

Discuss some or all of the following:

1. How might John 6 (feeding the five thousand) relate to the Eucharist?

2. What examples can be suggested of Jesus *eating* with people?

3. How can we *prepare* for Sunday Mass during the week?

4. How can we describe the difference between 'going to Mass' and '*experiencing* the Eucharist'?

5. What is meant by 'our need to respond'?

6. Which symbols (including words and gestures) do you find helpful/confusing?

7. What changes might be suggested which could help our understanding of the meaning of Mass?

8. Do any of the following seem to be given more or less emphasis at the Masses experienced by members:
   – sacrifice;
   – meal;
   – celebration;
   – community?

LARGE GROUP

Take any comments or questions from the Group.

After any practical matters have been dealt with, move into a time for prayer.

PRAYER

In a prayerful attitude, ponder on the four **actions** of the Liturgy of the Eucharist. Don't move on to the next until each one has 'said' all it can to you:

1. The priest **takes** bread and wine.

2. He gives God **thanks** for the bread and wine in the Eucharistic Prayer, and asks for God to bless the bread and wine, so that they become the Body and Blood of the Lord.

3. The priest **breaks** the bread.

4. The priest **gives** the Body and Blood to the disciples of today.

Conclude with everyone saying together the *Anima Christi*, or *Soul of Christ*:

> Soul of Christ, sanctify me.
> Body of Christ, fill me.
> Blood of Christ, save me.
> Water from the side of Christ, wash me.
> Passion of Jesus, strengthen me.
> O good Jesus, hear me.
> Let me not be separated from you.
> From the malicious enemy defend me.
> In the hour of my death, call me,
> and bid me come to you,
> that with your saints I may praise you
> for ever and ever.

(Pope John XXII, 1249-1334)

UNIT 15
Reconciliation, and Anointing of the Sick

Reconciliation (Penance)

Being a Christian involves the whole of our selves, the whole of our lives. God loved us into existence as whole beings, as precious, free, responsible living souls. We have been made responsible for all that we do in this world. God inspires and guides us, but the choices we make are ours. From the beginning, God's friendship, but not his interference, was offered. The created world was handed over to the care of free men and women. Had they chosen to follow the advice offered, Paradise, Eden, could still have been theirs.

Each person is able to recognise the Adam or Eve in his or her own life. We know only too well the story. Both Adam and Eve ate the fruit of the tree of [the knowledge of] good and evil, trying to make themselves like unto God. But they passed the buck to the serpent, a symbol of the pagan cultures which surrounded the people of God at that time. But God wasn't buying the buck passing. It stopped with Adam and Eve. It stops with us.
(*Helping Your Child to Know Right From Wrong*)

Time and again God takes the lead in restoring relationships broken by us: the Ten Commandments, the prophets, the Beatitudes – all to guide, not to force. Whilst respecting our freedom, God does not leave us unaided: the Holy Spirit dwells within us: God's grace unites us with him. Christ's Body, the Church, nourishes us with life-giving sacraments, provides us with supporting communities and helps us to be restored to wholeness when we have abused our freedom.

Jesus shows us how true freedom works. Despite extreme pressures, Jesus always exercises his free choice, in his case by choosing to do the will of his Father. In making this choice, he makes a choice for life, for full, absolute, eternal, wholeness of life. What of our choices? Do they lead us to life, or to 'other gods' – money, prestige, success, luxury?

Do we pour out our time and energy on others – the hungry, the sick, the imprisoned; working for social justice and world peace? Do the choices we make while shopping encourage animal cruelty (battery hens, factory farms, etc.), pollution of the environment, the exploitation of sweated labour? Do we choose to drink and drive? To evade tax? To fare-dodge? To waste company time? Do we work at building relationships within the family, the neighbourhood? Do we talk to our spouse, or just criticise? Do we grumble and depress those around us? . . . the list is endless.

Sometimes basic attitudes about ourselves can cause us to fall into traps which can poison our lives.

Three such traps:
Trap One
Believe that you *should* be perfect, exceptional.
Someone points out some little failing.
Fall – so you must be *worthless*: 'Poor me!'

Trap Two
Believe that you should be treated with considerable sympathy and consideration.
Someone fails to go out of their way for you.
Fall – so other people can be damned: 'Get lost!'

Trap Three
Believe that you should live a good, comfortable life.
Someone else lives a better, more comfortable life.
Fall – so the world can go hang, God doesn't care: 'Down with everything!'

(For a fuller treatment of this idea see *Fully Human, Fully Alive*, by John Powell S.J.)

The biggest trap of all is that of believing that we're too old, or too stubborn, or too set in our ways, to change. It's true – left to ourselves, we can't! We have to live with the consequences of our actions, but with God's help we can learn to overcome those sinful, selfish drives which often cause terrible effects. We can grow as people from the experience and, best of all, we can experience very personally the wonderful love and forgiveness with which God embraces us.

Too old, too stubborn or too set in our ways to change.

Through this highly personal sacrament [of Reconciliation] Christ continues to meet the men and women of our time. He restores wholeness where there was division, he communicates light where darkness reigned, and he gives a hope and a joy which this world could never give.
(Pope John Paul II, Liverpool, 1982)

When Jesus encountered those whom others called 'sinners', he reacted with what was thought of as 'shocking' behaviour! He did not scold, blame, or shun them. Instead he went home with them for meals, welcomed their friendship, offered them God's forgiveness. To him, they were 'strayed sheep', hurt or ignorant brothers and sisters. Even in his agony on the cross, he prayed: 'Father, forgive them! They do not know what they are doing.' He saw beyond people's sinful actions to the sort of people they *could* become. He showed that where love operates, there is no room for resentment, revenge, bitterness. New beginnings can be made, new life enjoyed.

Where love operates, people and God are brought back into friendship, reconciled. Where love operates, people will be reconciled with each other; systems of oppression, exploitation, greed and conflict can be radically overcome, the hunger for justice satisfied.

Jesus still encounters sinners, forgives them and brings them new life. He does it now through his Body on earth today, the Church. At his first appearance to the assembled disciples after his resurrection, he sent them out to continue his work of reconciling people with God and each other: 'Receive the Holy Spirit. For those whose sins you forgive, they are forgiven.' *(John 20:22-23)*

Through the power of the Holy Spirit, the Church continues Christ's work of reconciling the world to himself . . . handing on to others the gift that she herself has received, the gift of having been forgiven and made one with God.
(Pope John Paul II, Liverpool, 1982)

In the early years of the Church, the Sacrament of Reconciliation was allowed to be experienced only once in a lifetime, after baptism. People then tended to put off baptism for as long as possible! If you *did* commit a serious sin after baptism – murder for example, or betraying fellow Christians to the persecuting authorities – and you wanted to return to the Church, you were an **official penitent**. Penitents had to undergo rigorous trials to prove that they were truly sorry for harming the community by their serious sins.

When the community was convinced that the penitent was sincere, and would not betray or scandalise them, they would welcome them back into the Church with a joyful service of reconciliation led by the bishop.

By the thirteenth century, Irish monks had introduced the system of frequent, private confessions, so that in 1215, the Fourth Lateran Council obliged every Christian to confess and receive penance once a year. Later, more frequent confessions became standard practice. Since Vatican II it has been possible for the whole parish to celebrate together both the pain of knowing how harmful our lack of love can be for our relationship with God and each other, and the joy of experiencing our reconciliation.

These community celebrations, except for rare occasions, include the opportunity for individuals to go to a priest to confess in private and to hear through his words the wonderful forgiveness of God. Whether or not the community celebrates together, it is always represented by the priest, so that each person who has recognised his/her sinfulness and has turned to God, becomes reconciled both with God and with the community. When restored to wholeness, the Christian can be again an effective witness to the values of Christ Jesus and the love of God.

The Church provides choices in the way confession can be experienced. Some people prefer to *see* the priest when they confess, others to have a mesh or grill between them. Some people need to 'make a habit' of going regularly, even once a week, to reflect on their lives in the light of the Gospel; others prefer to wait until they have a serious matter to 'get off their chests' or when they have a choice of confessors. The Church recommends that people keep in touch with the practice of examining their consciences, and that they celebrate the sacrament at least once a year. Serious sin certainly needs attending to within the sacrament of confession whereas lesser sins committed, or minor good deeds not done, can be repented of and absolution received within *and by* the celebration of Mass and in prayer, particularly during the recitation of the Lord's Prayer.

Sin is not only that which I do myself, knowingly and wilfully, but that (injustice or corruption) which I allow to be done because I do nothing to stop it. The 'not doing good' is known as the sin of omission – of which all of us stand condemned in a society which knows genocide, torture, child abuse, cruelty to people and animals, environmental destruction and all the evils brought home to us daily on the news.

If we say we have no sin in us, we are deceiving ourselves and refusing to admit the truth; but if we acknowledge our sins, then God who is faithful and

just will forgive our sins and purify us from everything that is wrong.
(*1 John 1:8-9*)

Anointing of the Sick

Can we doubt God's concern and compassion for the sick, wounded and handicapped? Jesus spent much of his time healing – restoring sight, health to paralysed limbs and bodies ravaged by leprosy, repairing disturbed minds. He even caused life to return to dead bodies. His **healing miracles** were symbols of God's longing for our wholeness; words of tender love expressed in miraculous action. Today, God heals through the skills of doctors, nurses and medicines, as well as by the loving touch of caring relatives, friends and others. The faith community can also convey God's healing through the Sacrament of the Sick, a sacrament which 'should be approached in a spirit of great confidence . . . We must believe in Christ's healing love and reaffirm that nothing will separate us from that love. Surely Jesus wishes to say: "I will; be clean" (*Matthew 8:3*): be healed; be strong; be saved.' (John Paul II, Southwark Cathedral, 1982)

The **sign** used in this sacrament is one of anointing with **specially blessed** oil. This is the third time a Christian receives an anointing, after baptism and confirmation. For this reason it used to be called: 'Extreme Unction' or 'Last Anointing', but 'last' (of three) came to be understood as implying 'close to death'. Indeed the sight of a priest approaching for this sacrament was a source of fear which could prove fatal for a frail patient!

Since the Second Vatican Council, the emphasis on **healing** has been restored, the healing of the whole personality, body, mind and spirit. Part of the prayer accompanying the anointing, reads: 'Through this holy anointing and his great love for you, may the Lord help you by the power of his Holy Spirit. Amen. May the Lord who frees you from sin save you and raise you up.'

The sacrament is intended for the seriously ill, and for the elderly weak, and may be repeated as often as necessary. Whether or not a cure follows, the really important effect will have been the encounter or meeting with Christ brought about by this as with all the sacraments. A cause for celebration indeed! This can enable those who have to face death to do so with renewed courage and confidence. Death, which to us 'this side' may appear a disaster, yet is the door through which we all must go, knowing that beyond is the limitless love and splendour of God. Our present senses are inadequate to bear the full experience of perfect union with God. Death can be the 'ultimate healing event'.

As with reconciliation, the parish family can gather to express their faith, helping the sick by their prayerful support in communal services. The community of faith is also represented by the priest when he administers the sacrament in a home visit, or at the hospital. Lay people take Holy Communion to the sick, and often spend time with them, bringing them the news of the parish and providing often much needed company and support. A community which does not care for its members when they are sick or elderly, does not care for Christ Jesus, whatever fine words they might use.

Group Session

SMALL GROUPS

(*Note:* For this Session the Small Groups meet first.)

Welcome everyone; review the theme. Invite reflections; the leader may need to share first:

- Have we ever experienced the effects of conflict, division or prejudice?
- When and how have we personally experienced reconciliation with another and/or with God?
- What may be the 'other gods' in our lives? Are we aware of the consequences of the choices we make?
- In what areas is there the need for reconciliation in our community/world?
- How can we answer those who say 'Why did God let *this* happen?'

LARGE GROUP

The Leader explains the process involved in the Sacrament of Reconciliation. Invite questions and suggestions for ways in which the community can act to bring about unity and reconciliation in our world. What are the issues which cause division? Break for coffee/social gathering.

SMALL GROUPS

Discuss this statement of Pope John Paul II (at Southwark, 1982):

'Do not neglect the sick and elderly. Do not turn away from the handicapped and dying. Do not push them to the margins of society. For if you do, you fail to understand an important truth.'

- What did he mean?
- Have we experienced pain or loneliness? How were we supported?

'We begin by imagining that we are giving to them, and end by realising that they have enriched us.' (John Paul II)

- Have we ever found this to be so?
- How is the Christian's attitude to suffering and death different from that of an unbeliever's?

LARGE GROUP

· The Leader should explain the process involved in the Sacrament of the Sick. Invite questions and suggestions for how the parish community can keep the sick and handicapped at the centre of our lives. Could facilities be improved, more frequent visits made? After practical matters have been dealt with, move on to prayer.

PRAYER

In silence, with closed eyes,
either
– picture someone with whom you need to be **reconciled**:

see them standing close to Jesus, with Jesus calling to you to put your hand in theirs. Imagine Jesus has one arm around you, and one arm around that other person. Praise and thank him for the life of the other person.

or

– picture someone who is in need of Christ's **healing** – from physical or mental suffering. Pray for that person. See him/her as deeply loved by God who is near to them, suffering as they suffer. Praise and thank God for that person's life and for God's healing – whether or not it is manifested in the way that we expect.

After a time of mental prayer, invite those who wish to, to suggest the name of someone they would like the group to pray for. Conclude with everyone saying together this short medley of prayers:

Mark 1:40-42
A leper came to Jesus and pleaded on his knees: 'If you want to,' he said, 'you can cure me.' Feeling sorry for him Jesus stretched out his hand and touched him. 'Of course I want to!' he said. 'Be cured!' And the leprosy left him at once and he was cured.

An Act of Contrition
My God, I am sorry and ask forgiveness for my sins.
By the help of your grace I will try not to sin again.

Almighty, ever-living God,
whose love surpasses all that we ask or deserve,
open up for us the treasures of your mercy.
Forgive us all that weighs on our conscience,
and grant us more even than we dare to ask.
We make our prayer through Christ our Lord.
Amen.

UNIT 16
Orders
(Priesthood)
and Marriage

There are as many different ways of living life as a Christian as there are Christians. The Church is made up of all kinds of people – young and old, rich and poor, married and single. The important thing is that once a person has received the three Sacraments of Initiation, he or she is as much a full member of the Church as is a bishop or the Pope. The Church to which they belong has been given a job to do with regard to everyone in the world. This is called its **mission**. This is not so much to take Christ to the world, as he is already there, but to reach out in love to the people of the world, opening their eyes and hearts to God and drawing them into one family of brothers and sisters.

To accomplish its mission, the Church must show itself to be a kind of visual aid: it must be seen to be a body of people who live lives of loving service, otherwise all its talk about love would be just empty words. When people are aware of God's Spirit in their lives, they experience a deep need and longing to explore this with others and to join others in expressing their praise and thanksgiving. It is the Church's privilege to provide the opportunity for the worship of God, and particularly in its most perfect expression of thanksgiving, the Eucharist. No matter who a person is, as a member of the Church there must be some visible evidence that something of this activity is happening in his or her life. As the old saying goes: 'If you were arrested for being a Christian, would there be enough evidence to convict you?'

Everyone who is a member of the Church shares in the Church's mission. For this reason every member of the Church can be called a 'priest', meaning a person who leads a life of service for others. However, there are different ways of being a priest. We have in the Church people who choose to marry; those who live their lives as single people, and those who are 'ordained'. They are all sharing in the mission of the Church, but in different ways.

The Ordained Priesthood

Some people in the Church become its public servants through what is called 'Holy Orders', by being **ordained**.

Those ordained include bishops, priests and deacons.

A **deacon** can be a man in his final year of preparing to become a priest, or he can be a permanent deacon, in which case he can be a married man and can be in full-time secular employment.

What do deacons do?

A deacon's service is threefold, involving liturgy, the word, and charity. Liturgically he may preside at baptisms, weddings and funerals, and lead the people in prayer; proclaiming the word, he may read the Gospel and preach; for charity, he serves the needs of the people, especially of the poor, from right within the heart of the people. A deacon is ordained to assist the bishop, who may then require that he undertake chaplaincy, parish or wider work.

A **priest** is under the authority of either a bishop or, if he is also in Religious Orders, a superior. With a few exceptions, all priests in the Western Church are required to be and remain celibate (= single). In a sense their lives become public property and they become accountable to the rest of the Church. In a way they are the public face of the institutional side of the Church.

Their tasks include:

- proclaiming the Word of God – to present the message of God's love and to enable people to explore their lives in terms of the Gospel;
- helping, with others, to build up the Christian community;
- reaching out in service to the world outside the Church;
- leading the Christian community in worship, presiding at the Eucharist, and pronouncing God's pardon for sin to those who turn to him.

Down the ages there have been different ways of looking at this priesthood. Sometimes a priest was seen to be a kind of **judge**, the man who upheld the rules in the Church. At other times he was simply the man who **did holy things**, looked after the 'worship' side of life, the man who acted as the go-between with God and humankind. Other ages have seen him as the Guru, the **wise and holy man.**

All in all it is impossible to define exactly what the ordained priest is and does, because his life touches closely on the 'mystery' which is at the heart of the Church, i.e. the mysterious presence of God.

Collaboration

Nowadays, priests share much of their work with lay people, 'collaborative ministry' (priests, deacons and lay people all working together) becoming an increasing feature in parish and diocesan life. The Church recognises that the gifts of all people, young and old, male and female, are needed both to build up the Church and to serve the world. The range of activity expected of priests is markedly different from what was customary in times past. Often one of a 'team' with members of his parish, the priest can nevertheless look to the New Testament for models of his role in the Church:

First he is a **disciple**, that is, he has heard the call from Jesus to 'follow me'. So his job is called a **vocation**. Being a disciple is the priest's whole life; he cannot be a part-timer.

Secondly, he is an **apostle**. That means he is *sent* to serve others. His concern is for all people, not only for the Catholics in his parish. As an apostle too he is sent with authority to preach the Gospel.

Thirdly, he is a **presbyter**. That means he has a pastoral care for a group of people. It is his job to organise and stabilise a community. His authority over them is not one of domination, but of service. He represents the wider Church to them, as he is the local bishop's representative and delegate. While he may work closely with lay parishioners, he it is who is accountable to the bishop for the care of his parish.

Finally, he **presides** for them: he gathers them together around a table or altar at which he consecrates elements of food and drink for the sacred meal through which God and people become one. In the person of Christ he absolves repentant people of their sins and anoints the sick and dying.

In other words the priest acts in the name of Christ. It is Christ's mission in which he shares, that of building up the Body of Christ.

Two Questions

Why cannot priests marry?

This is a matter which the Church can change if the authorities wish, but of which there seems little sign at present, despite much debate. Reasons for celibacy include the following:

'Celibacy is one of the ways in which the priest takes on the undivided heart of Jesus himself. It is a challenge to love at the deepest level, a love without limits and open for all, a love which makes present the gentle power of the love of God. Celibacy is an opportunity to be really free in one's service of others. When lived in love for Jesus Christ, it gives the priest an inner freedom to cherish God's people with the love of the Good Shepherd. It leaves him totally open and available for those he serves, and free to move to wherever he can best be of service.' (*A Catholic Priest: Today and Tomorrow*, Michael Evans, Committee for Ministerial Formation, Bishops' Conference of England and Wales, 1993, p.28)

Why not ordain women priests?

Women share with men the 'common priesthood' of all the baptised, but they cannot be ordained into the sacramental priesthood. The authorities of the Catholic Church feel that they are not competent to authorise a change from the 'unbroken tradition throughout the history of the Church Universal in the East and in the West.' (Declaration: *Inter insigniores*, 'Women and the Priesthood', 1976.) The precedence of Christ appointing only men as apostles is often invoked, although the Pontifical Biblical Commission did not find the New Testament evidence to be decisive either for or against women's ordination. Symbolic language provides an argument against women as priests in that the priest presides over the liturgy as the symbol of Christ himself (*in persona Christi*), the bridegroom of the Church (see *Ephesians 5:29-32*). Thus the need for 'natural resemblance' between Christ and the person who is his sign suggests that only men can fulfil that.

Marriage

Since God is intimately present in the world he has created there are certain 'mysterious' things which we do that bring us into closer contact with this mystery or presence of God in the world. Birth, death, marriage, sickness, eating/drinking: in all these activities it is possible to sense God's plan for the world being worked out. Marriage is an important part of this mystery. In many ways it makes plain what the Church is all about. It acts again like a visual aid. The official Church could talk for all eternity about love and service, but unless we can see these things being lived out somewhere in flesh and blood, then we are tempted to believe they are fairy tales.

When two people commit themselves, in the presence of the Church's minister and the parish community, to live together in love until death, they are promising to do something which is of great benefit for everyone else in the Church. Here in the lives of this pair we can see all sorts of things being acted out:

- They promise to **belong** to each other: to work at belonging to one another, so that in a sense they cease to be two different people, and become one unity. Their individual personalities can develop with the support of a loving relationship.
- They learn to **forgive** each other. They show that reconciliation, which is part of the mystery of the Church's mission, is possible. In this they are similar to the priest, whose job it is to reconcile all manner of different parts of the human family to God.
- They bring **healing** to each other. All the hurts and damage which early life may bring can be repaired in the unconditional love which the couple has for each other. In many ways this is a second chance at meeting the unconditional love which parents have for their children.
- They share **joy**. They delight in each other, and so prove that the happiness of one can be increased by forgetting self and living to make another happy.

Marriage is also living proof of the cross. In real relationships, unlike those in story books, selfishness can be found with self-giving, the wish to dominate or wield power with generous love and the wounding word or silence at times replacing healing. This is precisely the same kind of tension in which all manner of Christian forms of service are lived out.

The specific issues of sexual morality which belong to marriage are dealt with in Unit 17. Here it is sufficient to see marriage as one of the ways in which the healing/reconciling work of Christ is carried out in the world today.

Can Catholics remarry?

If, after marital breakdown, a Catholic obtains a divorce, he or she is in no way barred from the Catholic community or from sharing fully in the sacraments. Before marrying again, however, the Church, through its marriage tribunals, needs to consider whether the previous marriage had been a valid one or not. If not, then an annulment can be granted and the person may then marry (as if for the first time) and take a full part in every aspect of Church life. If the previous marriage was deemed to be valid, or if no annulment has been sought, then any second or further marriage cannot be considered valid. People in such an invalid union are full members of the Church in every respect but one: they cannot take Communion at Mass, though they can present themselves for a blessing. The Church wishes to do two things at once: to uphold and encourage the sanctity of marriage – with its lifelong commitment – and to offer care and support to those who have suffered the pain of marital breakdown.

Group Session

LARGE GROUP

Welcome everyone; review the theme. The Leader should explain briefly the relationship between bishop and priest, priest and deacon – i.e. what each specifically does; how their roles differ, overlap and complement, etc.

If a priest is presenting this part of the session, he could share those aspects of the priestly ministry which he finds most gratifying. What might be stressed in encouraging vocations?

If members of religious orders (or third orders) are present, invite them to share briefly their particular 'apostolate'.

Discuss how marriage preparation is undertaken in the parish. Could it be improved? (See also the Unit on Love, Sex and the Church.) Explain the work of Marriage Care (formerly the Catholic Marriage Advisory Council) and/or Marriage Encounter. If possible, also mention Engaged Encounter and/or Choice weekends.

SMALL GROUPS

Questions for discussion:

- In his book *To Be a Pilgrim*, Cardinal Hume says: 'Most marriages last and are happy, but all marriages could be better.' Do you agree? How would you answer 'How?'
- Cardinal Hume also says that 'Holiness consists in doing ordinary things extraordinarily well'. What might he mean? Which *ordinary* things, and how?

. . . doing ordinary things extraordinarily well . . .

- Have we tended to leave **priestly ministry** or the striving for holiness, to the 'professionals', the 'uniformed branch' of the Church? In what ways can we share in Christian priesthood in our everyday lives? Is it possible in your situation to proclaim the faith, serve the world, and worship God?

- What is the role of **single people** in our parish? How do we care for the particular needs of the (often lonely) single people:
  - widows/widowers
  - divorced/separated
  - those who have never been married

How do they spend Christmas? Can they holiday with others? Do they always eat alone, especially Sunday lunch? Are they accompanied to parish socials? Does the single parent receive the special help he/she may need?

LARGE GROUP

Deal with any questions and comments from the Groups.

During discussion, have any ideas emerged on which positive action could be promoted and arranged? Could wedding anniversaries be celebrated liturgically? Would that be helpful? Perhaps 'Renewal of Marriage Vows' could be arranged? What action can the parish take concerning the interests of single people? Do prayers (e.g. the *Prayers of the Faithful*) ever take account of their situation?

When appropriate, move into a time of prayer.

PRAYER

With or without rosaries, use this time to say a **decade**, reading the Scripture passage as suggested, and possibly concentrating on the prayer suggested with each:

Joyful Mysteries

1. The Annunciation of the Angel Gabriel to Mary – *Luke 1:26-38.*
   'Speak, Yahweh [God], your servant is listening.' *1 Samuel 3:11.*
2. The Visitation of Mary to Elizabeth – *Luke 1:39-45.*
   'That I may truly believe that the promises made to me by the Lord will be fulfilled.'
3. The Birth of Jesus – *Luke 2:1-20; John 1:14.*
   'May Christ be born in my life this, and every, day.'
4. The Presentation in the Temple – *Luke 2:22-35.*
   'Praise God for his plan for my life.'

5. The Finding of the Child Jesus in the Temple – *Luke 2:41-52*.
'Lord, teach me how to listen, to question and grow in wisdom.'

Conclude with everyone saying together:

Let us pray
for all those who are in great difficulty –
for those who have lost their faith
in people and in love, their faith in God,
for those who seek Truth and cannot find it.
Let us pray for married people
who have drifted apart from each other
and for all priests who have broken down
under the strain of their office.

(Huub Oosterhuis)

UNIT 17
Love, Sex and the Church

A Christian chooses to follow Christ. That is the basic decision which determines the whole direction of a Christian's life. Every action and daily decision is inspired by the life and message of the person of Jesus Christ. Choosing, in the details of every day, a way of behaving which is Christ-like is far more than simply 'following rules', checking up on what is allowed or not, what is sinful or not. Personal relationships involve a morality which is consistent with Christ-like behaviour.

Morality is a call to advance in the direction of what is good – ultimately, that is, in the direction of God.
(Cardinal L. J. Suenens, *Christian Love and Human Sexuality*)

Really loving relationships between men and women require a high degree of generosity, constancy and unselfishness. Fortunes are rarely made from promoting such qualities as these. There are courageous Christians who are pilloried by the media and society for not worshipping at the shrine of self-indulgent sex. Authentic Christianity will always be a 'sign of contradiction' in societies which promote other gods – money, success, power. The deep anxieties which many, particularly young people, have about sex makes them easy prey for those who can exploit these fears and turn them into cash. Much of the advertising and entertainment industries thrive in this area.

Whole cultures can be so steeped in 'machismo' (an overbearing attitude of masculine 'superiority') as to coarsen and brutalise the human personality and prevent real relationships of love. Love, for a Christian, is not a game, a contest or a chance to dominate. Everyone is called to love, regardless of the sexual element, and authentic Christian love, modelled on that shown by Jesus, is based on respect for the other and concern for their happiness. All Christian morality is founded on this principle.

Moral norms

In order to be able to make right decisions in the field of relationships, as in other matters, a Christian should be aware of what God has said, both in Scripture and in the teaching office (the **Magisterium**) of the Church. We have not been left in the dark to guess, or simply to 'follow our feelings' (such notoriously unreliable guides). The Church has a long history of helping us to make the sort of decisions which ultimately safeguard our own, and other people's, welfare and happiness. The way the Church teaches is by offering firm guidelines, or 'moral norms'. A moral norm is 'not primarily a restriction or a prohibition. It is in the nature of a signpost or a map or a fence which prevents a disastrous fall.' (Cardinal Suenens, *Christian Love . . .*)

These teachings tend to be of a general nature, and cannot account for every detail of individual circumstance. Ultimately then, each person has the responsibility to consider each situation, prayerfully and carefully, reflecting on the concrete experience in the light of Christian principles and their own obligations and commitments. Only then can our consciences be satisfied that we are doing the right things in our circumstances. And it is according to our consciences that we will be judged 'on the day when God, through Jesus Christ, judges the secrets of mankind'. (*Romans 2:16*)

Deep within their conscience individuals discover a law which they do not make for themselves but which they are bound to obey, whose voice, ever summoning them to love and do what is good and to avoid evil, rings in their heart: Do this, keep away from that.
(*Pastoral Constitution on the Church in the Modern World*, n. 16, Vatican II)

Sexual behaviour

As the sexual instinct is one of life's most powerful forces, the Christian is naturally concerned to control it responsibly, and not be mastered by it. What can never be lost sight of, for the Christian, is that sexual behaviour should operate only within the context of a stable, loving relationship. To separate sex from love is to do violence to the whole complex unity of the human person. At two extremes, pornography is to authentic sexuality what sloppy romanticism is to love – they are both cheap counterfeits, selling people short because they are not the real thing. Marriage is the appropriate relationship for the 'real thing'. The total lifetime commitment of two people for each other is the right context for the expression of their total love for each other – **sexual, emotional** and **intellectual**. Within the stability and warmth of that relationship new life can most happily blossom and mature. Intimate sexual activity is therefore reserved exclusively for married partners. This may seem hard on all others – although there are many times even within marriage when physical self-control, chastity, is needed. Whereas for the unmarried, the physical sexual expression of love is inappropriate, there is for them no less the call to love and be loved, to respond to others with generosity and unselfishness.

Love, by its very nature, is **life-giving**. The Creator's love brought forth creation. Love cannot be closed in on itself, or it would cease to be, and become merely the mutual using of the other for personal wants and desires. Married love therefore can be expressed most fully through the bringing to life of children. Parents have the great privilege of co-operating with God's creativity in the building up of families. They have the responsibility and the right to plan their families, as Pope John Paul II taught during his visit to Brazil in 1980. In doing so they are to avoid being influenced by 'the spread of a contraceptive and anti-life mentality'. (Pope John Paul's address at York, 1982)

The Church teaches **responsible parenthood**, but the only method of family planning which receives her approval is the 'safe period'. This is because the cycle of fertility and infertility in the wife is part of God's deliberate creation, and to take advantage of it does not conflict with the Natural Law in the way that contraception does. In recent years, research has made it far easier to make an accurate assessment of when the fertile period will occur.

The Church has declared her beliefs on the morality of artificial birth control very clearly. But this is not the same as automatically labelling people who do not follow them as 'sinners', or determining the degree of blame incurred by individuals. Indeed this principle (of 'not judging') applies right across the moral field. Each of us is intimately answerable to God, who speaks to us with the voice of a trained conscience. The job of a Catholic is, then, to 'form' his or her conscience to the very best of his or her ability, according to the Church's teaching.

Life and death

All life is a gift of God. All living creatures therefore, are special, sacred and precious. God shared our human life in the person of Jesus. All human life then, must be respected and protected absolutely from the moment of conception.

The Church condemns all direct and intentional killing or anything which indirectly but intentionally brings about a person's death. (The only exceptions are in certain cases of self-defence or of legitimate defence of another's life or others' lives.) The principle is always the primacy of love and the sacredness of life. Genetic experiments on unborn babies or the destruction or harm of any embryo, other than by purely natural and unintentional causes, is considered to be anti-life, and so, unacceptable. This logically should extend to any action which harms the body, the 'Temple of the Holy Spirit', or the mind: self-inflicted ill-health caused by smoking, excessive eating or drinking; reckless driving and unnecessary risk-taking; drug-taking and sexual promiscuity; pollution of the mind through deliberate exposure to pornography or sensationalism ... all things which prevent the fulfilment of the human potential.

. . . unnecessary risk-taking . . .

There is a very great responsibility on Christians, one which their critics look for with often justified cynicism, that these values should not be just upheld and defended, but made to work. This can only be done with great sensitivity, love and sacrifice. It is not enough to *condemn* abortion – if a woman is to give birth instead she will need to be supported and warmly befriended. For the potential suicide to benefit from counselling she/he needs similar support and befriending. The Christian cannot honestly pray for good health whilst not taking steps to live healthily. The Christian community must seriously engage in the hard, but rewarding, work involved in improving the quality of life for all people, and in prophetically denouncing any attitude or behaviour which lowers or destroys human dignity. Christians should be people renowned for their sympathy, kindness and understanding; those who are the first to forgive; those who are patently reliable, honest and genuine. Then others will be drawn to recognise that Christians really *live out* their claim to believe in the sanctity of life.

Group Session

LARGE GROUP

Welcome everyone; review the theme. Invite representatives of parish organisations (such as Life, S.P.U.C. and Marriage Care) to describe their activities.

Catholic secondary schools are often willing to lend films, audiovisual materials, etc., on sex education.

Invite discussion on those issues raised in the Introduction about which members feel concerned. Few moral questions are simple or straightforward in real life: what stories can be shared to bring out the issues involved?

SMALL GROUPS

Any or all of the following questions may be helpful in developing discussion:

1. Can any stories be remembered of Jesus' treatment of sin and sinners?

2. 'The Church should just tell us what to do. Our job is just to obey.' How would you respond to this statement?

3. How might someone have to make a choice between two actions, neither of which is good? Would they inevitably be committing sin?

4. Can conscience be wrong? How can we help ourselves/our children to form a true conscience?

5. How far can the Ten Commandments be seen as expressing the law of love?

6. What elements would you like to see covered in an 'education for maturity' programme in schools?

7. Is it ever possible to judge the extent of another person's sin?

8. Do these words of St Paul have meaning for you: 'I cannot understand my own behaviour. I fail to carry out the things I want to do, and I find myself doing the very things I hate.' (*Romans 7:15*)

9. Does 'Thou shall not' sum up Christian moral principles?

10. If the fact concerns us that one in every five pregnancies in the U.K. ends in abortion (currently 180,000 each year) what can we do about it?

LARGE GROUP

What action can the parish, or groups within the parish, take to support those who are faced with difficult moral decisions?

After practical matters have been dealt with, move on to prayer.

PRAYER

When all are in the appropriate attitude for prayer, the Leader should guide the thoughts of those present back through their lives to times when they have felt hurt, wounded psychologically and emotionally. Ask them to hold onto that painful moment for a time, while the following passage is read aloud slowly: *John 8:34-36.*

Ask our Lord to heal that hurt, to set you free. Know that that pain has now been handed over. Feel that the space left is being filled with warm, life-giving love. Praise and thank God for his healing touch.

Conclude with everyone saying together:

God be in my head
and in my understanding.
God be in mine eyes
and in my looking.
God be in my mouth
and in my speaking.
God be in my heart
and in my thinking.
God be at mine end
and at my departing.

(*Sarum Primer*, 1527)

UNIT 18
Justice and Peace

At the centre of Jesus' teaching lies: **The kingdom of God**. What sort of kingdom does he mean? Not the sort of kingdom, surely, which is remembered during the annual telling of the Passover story – the harsh, tyrannical kingdom of the Pharaohs?

No, God's kingdom means freedom from that; it means: 'good news to the poor, liberty to the captives, to the blind, new sight, to set the downtrodden free – to proclaim the Jubilee' (see *Luke 4, Isaiah 61* and *Leviticus 25*). (The Jubilee was the 50th year, when slaves were freed, debts wiped out and land leases expired, which avoided land monopoly falling into the hands of a few. God was understood as owning all land, with us as his tenants, stewards of God's world.) This describes the kingdom for which Jesus lived, and died. Its aim is to promote the kind of life for which people were made – the life of a free people, loving God above all things, and keeping God's commandments. The wandering, ragged group of ex-slaves whom God chose to show to the world this radically different sort of kingship was simply 'the least of all peoples' (*Deuteronomy 7:7*). The 'least of people' – the poor, the strangers, widows, orphans (today we refer to these people as 'those on the margins of society'), have always been God's special ones, heirs to God's kingdom. 'Yahweh, forever faithful, gives justice to those denied it, gives food to the hungry, gives liberty to prisoners.' (*Psalm 146:6-7*)

People forget the lessons of history

The Israelites, rejecting the kingship of God (*1 Samuel 8:7*), clamoured for a king 'like the other nations' (verse 5). But their third king, Solomon, behaved so like a Pharaoh that he left a country split and in conflict for generations. Eventually, foreign domination and exile brought that to an end. By the time of Christ, Israel, under Roman rule, bred various groups all seeking in their own way to re-establish the kingdom of God:

– the **Pharisees**, by the legalistic, scrupulous practice of religion;

- the **Essenes**, by leading lives in communities separated from the 'ungodly';
- the **Zealots**, by attempting desperate acts of armed struggle (which finally brought about the destruction of Jerusalem, widespread massacres and forced exiles);
- and, the **Sadducees**, by appeasing the authorities and trying not to 'rock the boat' (in which they were positioned rather comfortably!).

Into this scene came a poor, pacifist layman from Nazareth, who mixed with sinners and outcasts, and chose uneducated peasants, fisherman and women to be his friends and followers. The Son of God 'emptied himself to assume the conditions of a slave' (*Philippians 2:7*). The Christ came from a long line of the **anawim**, the poor of Yahweh, the socially powerless who depended on God alone. Jesus, who broke down the barriers between Jew and Gentile, male and female, slave and free (*Galatians 3:28*), created a new relationship between people, making all people brothers and sisters of one another, with him and so with God. How we treat the least of our brothers and sisters will ultimately be seen as the way we have treated Christ (*Matthew 25:31-46*) – so closely does he identify himself with the poor and the oppressed of the world.

Every time we celebrate the Eucharist, sharing in the body broken, and in the blood poured out for us, we are opening ourselves to be transformed. We are asking for the strength to be weak and vulnerable. We are committing ourselves to sacrifice (= make holy) our lives in the service of others. But, through the gift of the Spirit, we are also sharing in Christ's power to give life to the world, to establish the kingdom. Like Christ, as fellow-heirs to the kingdom, our 'kingly' service will be in 'washing the feet' of our neighbour.

The cultural change which we are calling for demands from everyone the courage to adopt a new lifestyle, consisting in making practical choices – at the personal, family, social and

international level – on the basis of a correct scale of values: the primacy of being over having, of the person over things.'
(Pope John Paul II, *Evangelium Vitae* encyclical)

Like the prophets and like Christ, we are called to stand back at times from the world, to reflect on it, to assess its values. Our own lives too need to be judged against the standards of the Gospel. This can be painful! 'The word of God . . . cuts like any double-edged sword but more finely.' (*Hebrews 4:12*) There is no promise here of the comfortable, self-satisfied, nice sort of feeling which passes for 'peace', for 'really it could be a complete denial of what Christ meant by peace which sent most of the apostles to brutal death and was a terrific confrontation with the society in which they lived'. (Dom T. Cullinan O.S.B. in *The Roots of Social Injustice*)

The society in which we all live involves us as participants. None of us is a mere 'spectator'. We cannot hide from our responsibilities to the world's poor and oppressed by barricading ourselves into our 'private worlds' – for there is only *one* world, God's, in which we are but tenants. Over the centuries we have created systems – economic, political, social and so on – through which only a few enjoy the benefits of the world's resources. When the Church speaks up for oppressed people anywhere, she is not 'dabbling in politics', but exercising her prophetic voice.

The earth has enough for everyone's need, but not enough for everyone's greed.
(Mahatma Gandhi)

Helder Camara (a former bishop in Brazil and a leading figure in the fight for peace and justice) notes the connection between 'structural violence' of systems which keep people poor, deprived and oppressed, and the (often bloody) violence of those victims, in response. Often one form of tyranny is simply exchanged for another, and is itself frequently met by violent state repression.

With as much money being spent on arms in the world as on health and education together, and with three-quarters of all arms sales going to the poorest countries, the Christian commitment to justice and peace must be absolute. As Pope John Paul II explained in his encyclical *Redemptor Hominis*, n. 16: 'We all know well that the areas of misery and hunger on our globe could have been made fertile in a short time, if the gigantic investments for armaments at the service of war and destruction had been changed into investment for food at the service of life'.

Our responsibility: our response

We ask: 'What can we do?' The answer might include the slogan: 'Live simply, that others may simply live.'

- It might involve our avoiding buying certain goods which have been produced at the cost of human or animal suffering.
- It might involve dropping an inflationary pay claim which causes prices to rise above the buying power of the poor, or puts others out of work.
- It might involve 'acting . . . against all forms of domination, slavery, discrimination, violence . . . and whatever attacks life' (John Paul II addressing Puebla conference, 1979). 'Whatever diminishes, enslaves or negates man is an offence against human dignity; it is also a kind of blasphemy against God.' (Cardinal Hume to the Church of England Synod)

The greatest challenge of the day is how to bring about a revolution of the heart, a revolution which has to start with each one of us. When we begin to take the lowest place, to wash the feet of others, to love our brothers with that burning love, that passion, which led to the Cross, then we can truly say, 'Now I have begun'.
(Dorothy Day, quoted in *Peacenotes No. 4*)

- It might involve taking a more responsible part in community life, in the Church, in Trade Unions, in political parties, in organisations and charities, in education programmes.
- It might involve restructuring our businesses and companies, devising new economic structures and breaking barriers between management and workers.
- It might involve giving 'witness on behalf of justice by offering non-violent solutions in areas of social conflict' (*Justice in the World*, Synod of Bishops, 1971).
- It might mean giving to charity, sharing our goods and time, while bearing in mind: 'You are not making a gift of your possessions to the poor person, you are simply handing over to him what is his. For what has been given in common, for the use of all, you have taken for yourself. The world is given to all, and not only to the rich.' (St Ambrose of Milan, fourth century, in *de Nabuthne*)

The poor, our brothers and sisters

Another fourth-century Church Father tells us to act *now*: 'What keeps you from giving now? Isn't the poor man there? . . . The command is clear; the hungry man is dying now, the naked man is freezing now, the man in debt is beaten now, and you want to wait until tomorrow? . . . If everyone took only what he needed and gave the rest to those in need, there would be no such thing as rich and poor. After all, didn't you come into life naked, and won't you return naked to the earth? . . . You do wrong to everyone you could help, but fail to help.' (St Basil)

The final word is given to Pope John Paul II in an extract from his speech in the Yankee Stadium in 1979: 'When we Christians make Jesus Christ the centre of our feelings and our thoughts, we do not turn away from people and their needs . . . The poor of the world are your brothers and sisters in Christ. You must never be content to leave them just the crumbs from the feast. You must take of your substance, and not just of your abundance, in order to help them.'

The poor of the world are your brothers and sisters in Christ

Group Session

LARGE GROUP

Welcome everyone; review the theme. Read together Isaiah 58:7-10. Invite representatives from agencies within the parish to give thumbnail sketches of their activities: *Justice & Peace group, Pax Christi, Christian CND, Cafod*, etc.

Invite members of the community who are involved in related agencies to outline their work – in politics, business, unions, government departments, charities, etc.

Discuss those areas of need most keenly felt by members, and see what the Church's role can be, for example in housing; unemployment; health care; immigration; needs of the handicapped; age, sex or racial discrimination.

SMALL GROUPS

Invite members to share stories of personal involvement in areas of injustice, discrimination, etc., or in areas of active concern for the poor, elderly, handicapped, etc.

Consider what may be the modern-day counterparts of the Pharisees, Essenes, Zealots and Sadducees, and the attitudes which underlie these positions.

Other topics for discussion:

- What do members understand by 'Christian Peace'?
- How reasonable are the items suggested on page 123 as possible answers to the 'What can we do?' question, and what others would members suggest?
- What, if anything, struck members in this Unit as new, provocative, helpful?
- Can members suggest any *one* new thing they may try to do *this week* as a result of this Unit?

LARGE GROUP

Take any comments and questions from the groups. After practical matters have been dealt with, move into prayer.

PRAYER

Throughout the world, at noon each day, thousands of people say this **Prayer for Peace**. Say it together now, pausing between each phrase to enable the words to 'strike home':

> Lead me from Death to Life,
> from Falsehood to Truth.
> Lead me from Despair to Hope,
> from Fear to Trust.
> Lead me from Hate to Love,
> from War to Peace.
> Let Peace fill our Heart,
> our World, our Universe.

(Satish Kumar)

Conclude with everyone saying together:

> Make us worthy, Lord, to serve our fellow
> men and women throughout the world,
> who live and die in poverty and hunger.
> Give them by our hands this day their daily bread,
> and by our understanding love give peace and joy.

(Pope Paul VI)

UNIT 19
Ecumenical and
Inter-Faith
Movements

Many older Catholics can remember when they were forbidden from worshipping with their Protestant neighbours. Although the modern ecumenical movement can be traced back to 1910, it was only with the Second Vatican Council that restrictions were lifted and Catholics encouraged to work and pray with other Christians for eventual unity. The Council Fathers also welcomed opportunities for Catholics to develop better relations with the followers of non-Christian religions. Centuries of mutual ignorance, intolerance and mistrust – even persecution – had to be sincerely repented of and the memories healed.

In the decades since the Council, enormous strides forward have been taken. Most Catholics now realise that ecumenism, or the 'bringing together of the one household of Christ' is not an 'extra', but a vital part of their Catholicism. 'Let no one delude himself that work for perfect unity is somehow secondary, optional, peripheral, something that can be indefinitely postponed.' (Pope John Paul II to Ecumenical Commissions, 23/11/79)

The restoration of the unity of all Christians was one of the principal aims of the Second Vatican Council, and reflects the will of Christ himself that 'all may be one' (*John 17*). Indeed, disunity is a scandal and a hindrance to the spread of the Gospel. The Church cannot fulfil its function of reconciling all people with each other and with God, when it is itself unreconciled and divided.

The demands of ecumenism are not satisfied just by a show of tolerance and goodwill. While disunity exists at any level, the painstaking work must go on – one step taken at a time, but taken by all.

Christian unity will be attained when the praying Christ has found enough Christian souls in all confessions in whom he himself can freely pray to the Father for unity.
(Couturier, quoted by E. Sullivan, in *Baptised into Hope*)

Unity does not mean 'sameness'. The variety of the Eastern Catholic Churches can testify to that. Whilst they differ among themselves in their liturgies, rules and spiritual traditions, yet this variety 'so far from diminishing the unity (of the Universal Church) rather serves to emphasise it'. (*Decree on Catholic Eastern Churches* n. 2)

The Catholic Church comprises twenty-three autonomous Churches, only one of which observes the Western, or Latin, Rite. The others observe specific rites derived from one of the six major Eastern Traditions: Alexandrian, Maronite, Syriac, Armenian, Chaldean and Byzantine.

The Orthodox Churches of the East have a different history both from those which remained in union with Rome, and from the Protestant Churches of the West. With no dispute on matters of sacraments, priesthood or the Eucharist, Catholics hope that 'with the removal of the wall dividing the Eastern and Western Church at last there may be but one dwelling, firmly established on the cornerstone, Christ Jesus, who will make both one'. (*Decree on Ecumenism* n. 18)

'Among those separated denominations in which Catholic traditions and institutions in part continue to exist, the Anglican Communion occupies a special place.' (*Decree on Ecumenism* n. 13) Successive Popes and Archbishops of Canterbury have expressed their common will to bring their communions into *one* communion of life, worship and mission: 'To this we are bound to look forward and to spare no effort to bring it closer: to be baptised into Christ is to be baptised into hope.' (Paul VI and Archbishop Coggan, Vatican 29/4/77) To achieve this, John Paul II and Archbishop Runcie (Accra, 9/5/80) urged that: 'The talents and resources of all the Churches must be shared if Christ is to be seen and heard effectively.'

Working together

Not only with Anglicans, but also with all the Protestant Churches, Catholics at every level are expected to work, pray and share. While theologians patiently try to solve the doctrinal problems, ordinary Christians are to do everything together, except that which conscience forbids. 'Teacup ecumenism is not to be despised . . . every occasion of friendly conversation with fellow Christians enables us to share perceptions of truth.' (Emmanuel Sullivan, *Baptised into Hope*)

Some of the things that local churches can do together are:

- 'covenant', pledge themselves to share resources and pool buildings, personnel and activities (see *Local Churches in Covenant*, booklet published by the Ecumenical Commission of England and Wales, 1982, recommended to all involved at local level);
- work together through organised Fraternals, Councils and Fellowships. These can run pulpit exchanges, 'awaydays', study days, socials, parties, prayer groups, etc.;
- jointly fund chaplaincies, schools and missions;
- promote Christian involvement in the media – local radio and TV and the press;
- foster groups of all Christians to study, either each other's traditions or matters of common interest, especially Scripture;
- undertake joint projects for social justice, such as housing, unemployment, race relations;
- plan together to care for the elderly, handicapped, housebound and others in need.

Behind all activities, must lie **prayer**: 'Prayer is at the origin of this movement; it accompanies, enlivens and sustains its effort.' (John Paul II, *Angelus*, 18/1/81) We do not have to wait for the annual Week of Prayer for Christian Unity. Pope John Paul II reminds us that *every* Mass is a privileged occasion for prayer for unity.

Unity achieved

While much has already been achieved, there still remains a great deal to do. The awareness of our incomplete unity is brought home to us painfully when we cannot receive Communion from, nor give it to, members of other Christian traditions. As the Bishops explained: 'It could be counterproductive to use what is the perfect symbol of unity achieved as a means of achieving it. This could defer indefinitely the full corporate union for which we all pray.' (*Easter People*, p. 77)

The Spirit of dialogue

The benefits to Christians of getting together with those of other religions and opening dialogue, or communication, with them, cannot be overstressed: 'May I suggest that we must not only listen to each other, but together listen to what the Spirit may be saying.' (Cardinal Hume to the Church of England Synod) Through this we discover how much we have in common with the other 'religions of the Book': Judaism and Islam.

Jews

The Second Vatican Council reminded Catholics that Christianity itself emerged from the root of Judaism, and that as St Paul himself says of his own people, the Jews: 'They were adopted as children, they were given the glory and the covenants; the Law and the ritual were drawn up for them, and the promises made to them. They are descended from the patriarchs and from their flesh and blood came Christ.' (*Romans 9, 4-5*)

Despite the close ties of faith between Christians and Jews, there has been a long history of misunderstanding and prejudice. Christians today acknowledge with shame and remorse the long record of crimes perpetrated against the Jewish people – pogroms and persecutions, killings and 'ethnic cleansing'. The Church requires Christians to be sensitive in the use of language, in interpretations of Scripture, in preaching and socially, not to give rise to, or to condone, any anti-Jewish sentiment or bias.

Since Christians and Jews have such a common spiritual heritage, this sacred Council wishes to encourage further mutual understanding and appreciation . . . by way of biblical and theological enquiry and through friendly discussions.
(*Declaration on the Church's Relation to non-Christian Religions (CRnCR)*, n. 4, Vatican II)

Muslims

'The Church has also a high regard for the Muslims . . . and the Council now pleads with all to forget the past, and urges that a sincere effort be made to achieve mutual understanding.' (CRnCR, n. 3)

The belief in the same one God, the common links with Abraham 'our forefather in faith', the honour which Muslims show to Jesus and his Mother, as well as their practice of prayer, alms-giving and fasting, help to bond Christians and Muslims in so many ways.

True and holy

As regards other major world religions: 'The Catholic Church rejects nothing of what is true and holy' in all the great religions which have inspired and guided people's lives. While in duty bound to proclaim Christ, in whom 'men find the fulness of their religious life', the Church yet urges Christians to 'enter with prudence and charity into discussions and collaboration with members of other religions. Let Christians, while witnessing to their own faith and way of life, acknowledge, preserve and encourage the spirit and moral truths found among non-Christians, also their social life and culture.' (CRnCR, n. 2)

Atheists

The Church is eager to enter into dialogue with different groups of people 'in order to achieve either a greater grasp of truth or more human relationships'. (Post-Vatican II Document *On dialogue with unbelievers*, 28/8/68) Among them are 'those who respect outstanding human values without realising who the author of those values is, as well as those who oppose the Church and persecute it in various ways. Since God the Father is the beginning and the end of all things; we are all called to be brothers; we ought to work together without violence and without deceit to build up the world in a spirit of genuine peace.' (*Church in the Modern World*, n. 92, Vatican II)

Group Session

LARGE GROUP

Welcome everyone; review the theme. Invite representatives of the local Churches Together to give examples of ecumenical action in the parish.

Invite members of the group to share insights into the admirable qualities found in followers of non-Catholic religious traditions.

SMALL GROUPS

Some or all of the following may be found helpful for group discussion:

1. To what extent have we inherited attitudes of resentment or mistrust towards followers of other religious traditions? What stirs up these feelings? What helps us to change them?
2. What is there in our language or behaviour which members of other faiths may find offensive or discriminatory? Have we ever been hurt in this way?
3. How justified are some Catholics in fearing that ecumenism may cause the submergence of Catholic identity? Of what may non-Catholics be fearful?
4. What are we doing to learn more about other religious traditions or Christian denominations? How important is it for us to understand the religious experience of others?

LARGE GROUP

Have a 'brainstorming' session in order to get from the group ideas about all the possible ways in which relations with other religious traditions may be fostered locally. Begin to plan which to put into operation immediately and which in the longer term.

After practical matters have been dealt with, move into prayer.

PRAYER

Read, or have read, slowly and meditatively, *John 17:11 'Holy Father . . .' up to verse 26.*
Conclude with everyone saying together the prayer which is held in common by most Christians of whatever denomination: *The Grace.*

May the grace of our Lord Jesus Christ,
the love of God and the fellowship of the Holy Spirit,
be with us all, now, and for evermore. Amen.

Unit 20
The Christian Response

We have been called: we are responding. We are asked to be open to God, and we accept. 'Do with me, Lord, as you will!' We offer our daily lives at the Offertory, represented by the products of our work and our wealth.

Goodness, do we know what we're doing! Just what may we be letting ourselves in for? There is always a risk that we may be taken at our word! There was the risk Jesus took in choosing disciples who may, one day, have betrayed him. There is the risk Jesus takes daily, in presenting himself so humbly and vulnerably as a small piece of bread. To receive the full rites of Christian initiation: baptism, confirmation and Holy Eucharist is to accept the **challenge** of the Gospel, to take on all the risks of forming ourselves into the image of Christ Jesus.

- When **Abraham** (Abram) was called, he had to leave the security of his homeland for the uncertainty of travelling with no reservations made! (*Genesis 12:1-5*)
- When **Moses** was called to liberate the Israelites, he ran the risk of incurring the tyrant Pharaoh's wrath.
- When **Mary** was called, she ran the risk of social disgrace and personal suffering.
- The **apostles** were called to follow Christ and to share the Good News with all people. This required commitment, dedication, total service, and, in many cases, their lives. Is less required of us? Since the New Testament was written, the acts of the apostles have been written in the lives of Christians – in their blood, their work, their prayers, their service, their love.

We are not all called to do everything. Fortunately for each of us, we simply make up the **Body of Christ**. But only when each of us does do, wholeheartedly and with love, what is asked of us, can that Body function effectively.

What is asked of us?

Our calling can be summed up by the three **Theological Virtues** (*1 Corinthians 13:13*):

faith –
we are called to intimate relationship with our God. We have the responsibility to nourish that relationship

through prayer, reflection and a sacramental life.

hope –

we are called to share the Good News with a needy world. We have the responsibility of being the image of God in the world today.

love –

we are called to love with God's love the world which he loved so much that he sent his only Son to die for it.

. . . since God has loved us so much, we too should love one another . . . as long as we love one another God will live in us and his love will be complete in us. (*1 John 4:11-12*)

Love is service

'Love' is not the vague, warm feeling we get when we think of someone. We are not even called to *like* our brother or sister! But we are called to *love* them. Jesus washed dirty feet as an example of love in action – action which was shortly to take on the deepest dimension in Jesus' own death on a cross.

To what **service** are we called? 'There are all sorts of service to be done.' (*1 Corinthians 12:5*)

Some service involves the **wider community**. This includes:

– teaching, nursing, social work,
– visiting the sick, housebound, imprisoned,
– involvement in local social and environmental improvement schemes,
– being active in national, local and union politics,
– being a good neighbour – hospitable, open, welcoming,
– being an honest worker, fair employer, good companion,
– making a happy home.

Some service is to the **parish community**. This includes:

– being a catechist with children, or adults,
– being a sponsor, being a Youth Leader,

- being a Parish Councillor or Pastoral Assistant,
- being a lift-giver, or baby-sitter, or care visitor,
- making the coffee after Mass, or collecting hymn books,
- running the parish charities and holding 'fund-raisers',
- organising social events and parish outings,
- seeing to communications.

Some service is to the **worshipping community** – the liturgical services. These include:

- being a Minister of Communion,
- being a Reader,
- being an Usher, or Welcomer, being a Server,
- being a Musician (organist, singer, guitarist, cantor, animator),
- being a 'Minister of the Environment' (flower arranger, cleaner, poster-maker, chair-mover, sacristan, and so on)

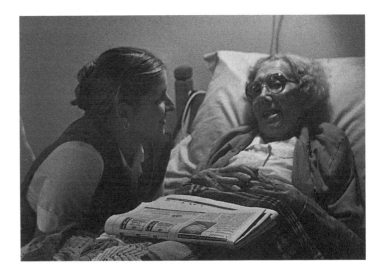

There is also the real service, performed by countless millions of elderly, housebound or sick people, that of **prayer** and **intercession**. Members of contemplative communities are as actively serving the Church and the world by their prayer as are the busiest of parish stalwarts, on committees for this and that, and bursting with good works!

Service, or ministry 'is a function of the *whole* Church. All Christians are ministers in virtue of the

Christ-life they have taken on in the rebirth of baptism.
. . . Whatever we as Christians are motivated or
inspired to do because of our baptism, then in doing it
we are helping to fulfil Christ's mission, spreading the
Good News.' (R. B. Kelly, ed., in *Called to Serve*)

Spreading the Good News is, after all, what the Church
is for. This is its purpose. 'Go out to the whole world;
proclaim the Good News to all creation.' (*Mark 16:15*)

Remember those mysterious gifts offered by the three
wise men to the infant Jesus? (*Matthew 2: 1-12*) – gold,
frankincense and myrrh. Their gifts were a recognition
that the Jesus they adored was **king** (gold), **priest** (use of
incense in liturgy) and destined to die a **prophet's**
violent death (myrrh, a burial spice). With the Sacrament
of Confirmation, the Christian is anointed to be an 'other
Christ', anointed therefore as priest, prophet and king.

This is no poetic fantasy:
  as shepherd-kings you are set apart
    to be responsible for others,
    to care for them,
    to lead them all into Truth;
  as priests you are commissioned
    to minister to others and to each other,
    to take the Word of Christ to them
    to live the life of Christ for them;
  as prophets you are called
    to speak out on behalf of others,
    to be fearless in opposing evil and wrong,
    at whatever cost,
    and, as myrrh signifies –
    for it speaks of death and burial,
    the cost is high.
  It can cost you all
    and that is what may be asked of you.
(from a *Pastoral Letter* by Bishop Alan Clark, Epiphany
1985)

This is no game. This is life.

Group Session

LARGE GROUP

Welcome everyone; review the theme. Read together, reflectively prepared sections of *1 Corinthians 12:12 – 13:13*.

Discuss the range of ministries available in the parish – liturgical and others.

SMALL GROUPS

Suggestions for discussion topics:

- In what ways can we offer service – to the parish? – to the community?
- What more could we do than we are doing?
- In what ways can we 'proclaim the Good News to all creation'?
- Why are there so few committed Christians in our society? How can we reach the others?
- Could we show more joy, love, and liveliness in our worship and in our relationships?
- If St Paul were to pay a visit to our parish, what might he later write to us?
- How can we continue to grow in faith, hope and love?

LARGE GROUP

Take any comments or questions from the groups.

Discuss 'Where do we go from here?' – forthcoming liturgical arrangements, follow-on sessions and so on. It may be a good moment to recruit volunteers or nominations for a range of ministries, or discuss how the parish can better support the existing ones.

After all the practical matters have been settled, try to spend some time in prayer.

PRAYER

Read, or have one person read aloud, *Matthew 4:16-20*, letting each phrase do its work.

Finally, conclude with everyone saying together the *Grail Prayer*:

Lord Jesus,
I give you my hands to do your work.
I give you my feet to go your way.
I give you my eyes to see as you do.
I give you my tongue to speak your words.
I give you my mind that you may think in me.
Above all, I give you my heart
that you may love in me your Father
and all mankind.
I give you my whole self that
you may grow in me,
so that it is you, Lord Jesus,
who live and work and pray in me.

POSTSCRIPT: R.C.I.A. – THE CHALLENGE TO THE CATHOLIC PARISH

When the Bishops at the Second Vatican Council promoted the R.C.I.A. (Rite of Christian Initiation of Adults) as their last reform, they were inviting the Church to take stock of itself and unleash a fresh new energy into its way of life.

The R.C.I.A. is radically new, yet draws extensively on the past, simply by opening up the treasures which the Church has long possessed. The primary focus is on the **would-be Catholic**. Yet the whole parish community is provoked into vital and critical self-examination:

- Is our parish attracting large numbers?
- Does it seem to be worth joining?
- What impression are we making on the world?
- How can we become the warm, welcoming, hospitable community in which our brothers and sisters can hear the Good News?

Where parishes have accepted the challenge of the R.C.I.A. they seem to find new life:

'The parish is charged with a new hospitality, an openness that was always there but not always viewed as a ministry. Evangelisation is just a word unless parishes restore the catechumenate. . . . Parishes that are not joining new members to their community around the table of the Lord are hiding the light that searches out the darkness, the healing spirit that challenges while it soothes.'
(R. Kemp, 'The Catechumenate and Parish Renewal', *New Catholic World*, 222:1329, p. 184)

Where to start

It may be helpful to make contact with a neighbouring parish in which R.C.I.A. is working. It *is* essential to buy the book of the Rites, and to study it closely. Bear in mind that your parish is unique and so are the people and the situations in it. You will need to adapt the Rites and all contributory material (like this book!) to your own needs. It is also essential to avoid 'going it alone'. This is the exercise *par excellence* in co-operation and lay responsibility. There is so much material available on the structure of the R.C.I.A. that only a sketch is appropriate here.

There are four unequal periods, or stages:
1. Pre-catechumenate
2. Catechumenate
3. Purification/intensification
4. Post-catechumenate (mystagogia)

Stage One (Pre-catechumenate)

– may have taken years. It applies to all who express any degree of interest or enquiry. They are called 'enquirers' and can simply observe and question. Should they feel drawn to want to find out in more depth how Catholics 'tick', with the view to becoming one themselves, they are welcomed into the **catechumenate** at an appropriate liturgical Rite of Welcome.

Stage Two (Catechumenate)

– may well take months or years. It all depends on the candidate and the community into which he/she wishes to be initiated. Supported by the prayers and companionship of the community (and especially the candidate's sponsor) the 'catechumen' follows the sort of programme of learning/sharing sessions which this book suggests. The second major step is for the candidate to make a serious commitment at the beginning of the Lent before the time when he/she will receive the full Rites of Initiation at or near the Easter Vigil.

Stage Three (Period of Purification, Enlightenment, Intensification)

– takes place over the weeks of Lent. Prayer, reflection, and liturgical support all help to prepare for the Big Moment. This comes at, or near, the Easter Vigil, when all the Rites of Initiation are experienced or completed.

Stage Four (Post-catechumenate, Mystagogia)

– is the 'follow-up' to the events at Easter. It is, most intensively, the period from Easter to Pentecost, when the Vigil experience is reflected upon, and the life of the community begun to be shared in fully. This period never really ends, as a life-time is too short to do justice to the task of growing and developing as a Christian.

The benefit to those who have travelled this path is acknowledged to be immeasurable:

'The first thing I learned was that I wasn't alone in my questions and searching. I met good people who besides sharing questions helped each other find new meaning and purpose to life and religion. The catechumenate was great, not because it gave me something I didn't have, but because it helped me find the God who was with me all along and helped me respond to God.'
(quoted in *Christian Initiation Resources*, Vol. 1, p. 20)

Who are 'sponsors', and what do they do?

The following is adapted from the invaluable and inexpensive *Guide for Sponsors*, by Ron Lewinski:

Each candidate or 'catechumen' is put in touch with a personal 'sponsor', probably the key person who led to their becoming interested in the first place – friend, spouse, neighbour, work-mate or similar.

If you are asked to be a sponsor, 'you will be the most direct or personal link the candidate will have to the community. You will not be expected to catechise a candidate but rather to share your faith and experience as a Catholic. The candidate will catch from you the life and spirit of the Church.' Your role is to be:

a companion, walking alongside the candidate throughout the preparation period;

a guide, pointing to the Lord as the destination of the journey;

a model of faith, to catch from you what being a Catholic is all about;

a witness for the community of the candidate's spiritual progress.

After Initiation, the community may choose a **godparent**, who may or may not be the sponsor, to continue to care for the new Catholic throughout the rest of his/her life.

Recommended Reading

The most useful compendium of Catholic doctrine to date is the official: *Catechism of the Catholic Church*, Geoffrey Chapman, 1994. It is best used as a reference book as occasions require.

Other useful reference books to have to hand are *The Modern Catholic Encyclopedia*, edited by Michael Glazier and Monika Hellwig, Gill & Macmillan Ltd, 1994, and *A-Z of the Catholic Church*, compiled by Luke Connaughton, Kevin Mayhew Ltd, revised edition 1997. Questions relating to Church Law may be settled by referring to the Canon Law Society's *The Canon Law, Letter and Spirit: a practical guide to the code of canon law*, Geoffrey Chapman, 1995.

For follow-up material for groups, the National Project of Catechesis and Religious Education, of the Bishops' Conference of England and Wales, has produced, among other useful resources: *'To live is to change', a way of reading Vatican II*, Rejoice Publications, 1995; and, *Parish Project: a resource book to help parishes to reflect on their mission*, HarperCollins, 1992.

For liturgical matters, a useful book is *Celebration: the Liturgy Handbook*, edited by Stephen Dean, Geoffrey Chapman 1993, a programme of study based on the *Syllabus for Liturgical Formation* published by the Liturgy Office of the Bishops' Conference of England and Wales.

BIBLIOGRAPHY

Further details of books referred to in the text.

Brown, R. E. *The Gospel according to St John*, Vol 1. Anchor Bible Series no. 29, Doubleday & Co., 1966, 1970.

Carretto, C. *Letters from the Desert*. Darton, Longman and Todd, 1972.

Christian Initiation Resources Vol 1. William Sadlier Inc., 1980-81.

Cullinan, T. *The Roots of Social Injustice*. C.H.A.S., 1973.

Eliot, T. S. *The Rock: a Pageant Play*. Faber & Faber, 1934.

Farrell, C. *Helping Your Child to Know Right from Wrong*. RPP Ligouri Publications, 1971.

Farrell, E. J. *Prayer is a hunger*. Dimension Books, N.J., 1972.

Fewell, M. *The Way We Were, Joppa*. T. Shand Publications, 1985.

Guzie, T. *The Book of Sacramental Basics*. Paulist press, 1981.

Kelly, R. B., ed. *Called to Serve*. Kevin Mayhew Ltd., 1985.

Konstant, D. *Jesus Christ: the Way, the Truth, the Life*. Collins, 1981.

Lewinksi, R. *Guide for Sponsors*. Liturgical Training Publications, 1980.

McKin, J. *Doorways to Christian Growth*. Winston Press Inc., 1984.

Martin, R. *Hungry for God*. Fontana/Collins, 1974.

O'Connor, B. *Celebration in Faith*. Austin Friars, Carlisle, 1982.

Peacenotes. Available from Pax Christi, St Francis of Assisi Centre, Pottery Lane, London W11.

Powell, J. *Fully Human, Fully Alive*. Tabor Publishing, 1976.

Powell, J. *Unconditional Love*. Tabor Publishing, 1978.

Purnell, A. P. *Our Faith Story*. Collins, 1985.

Rite of Christian Initiation of Adults: study edition, provisional text. Catholic Truth Society, 1974.

Sayers, S. *Focus the Word*. Kevin Mayhew Ltd, 1989.

Storey, W. G., ed. *Praise Him!* Ave Maria Press, 1973.

Sullivan, E. *Baptised into Hope*. S.P.C.K., 1980.

Suenens, Cardinal. *Christian Love and Human Sexuality*. C.T.S., S317, 1976.

Towards Adult Faith. Catholic Education Association of Australia, 1983.

ACKNOWLEDGEMENTS

The authors and publishers would like to thank the following publishers for permission to reproduce passages from the publications listed.

Ave Maria Press, Notre Dame, Indiana 46556, for the text of 'The Prayer of Abandonment' by Charles de Foucauld, from *Praise Him!* edited by W. G. Storey.

Catholic Adult Education Centre, Cnr. Howard & Rosslyn Streets, West Melbourne, Australia: *Towards Adult Faith*.

Catholic Housing Aid Society, 189a Old Brompton Road, London SW5 0AN: *The Roots of Social Injustice*, by T. Cullinan.

Catholic Truth Society, 38-40 Eccleston Square, London SW1V 1PD: *Christian Love and Human Sexuality*, by Cardinal Suenens.

Geoffrey Chapman, a division of Cassell Publishers, Ltd., Artillery House, Artillery Row, London SW1P 1RT, for the text of *Christ Be Beside Me*, by James Quinn, S.J.

Collins Publishers, 8 Grafton Street, London W1X 3LA: *Hungry for God*, by R. Martin; *Our Faith Story*, by A. P. Purnell; *Jesus Christ: the Way, the Truth, the Life*, by D. Konstant.

Darton, Longman & Todd Ltd., 89 Lillie Road, London SW6 1UD: *Letters from the Desert*, by C. Carretto; *The Jerusalem Bible*.

Doubleday & Co., 245 Park Avenue, New York, NY 10017, USA: *The Gospel according to St John*. Vol. 1.

Faber & Faber Ltd, 3 Queen Square, London WC1N 3AU for the extract from 'The Rock', taken from *Collected Poems 1909-1962*, by T. S. Elliot.

Ligouri Publications, Ligouri, Missouri 63057, USA: *Helping Your Child to Know Right from Wrong*, by Christopher Farrell.

Liturgy Training Publications, 1800 North Hermitage Avenue, Chicago, Illinois 60622-1101, USA: *Guide for Sponsors*, by Ron Lewenski. (Copyright Archdiocese of Chicago.)

Rev. B. O'Connor, O.S.A., Austin Friars School, Carlisle, Cumbria CA3 9PB: *Celebration in Faith*, by B. O'Connor.

Paulist Press, 997 Macarthur Boulevard, Mahweh, N.J. 07430, USA: *The Book of Sacramental Basics*, by Tad Guzie.

Prayer for Peace. The Prayer for Peace, by Satish Kumar, which has no ties with any single denomination or faith, is said daily at noon in many countries throughout the world and has been translated into more than 40 languages.

S.P.C.K., Holy Trinity Church, Marylebone Road, London NW1 4DV: *Baptised into Hope*, by E. Sullivan.

Tabor Publications, a division of DLM Inc., Allen, TX 75-002, USA: *Unconditional Love*, by John Powell, S.J.

Winston Press Inc., 430 Oak Grove, Minneapolis, Minnesota 55403, USA: *Doorways to Christian Growth*, by J. McKin.